THE SHADOW OF THE TEAPOT

To Beverley

Best Wishes
Margaret
x

January 2018

The shadow of the teapot is a true story, some names have been altered to protect the privacy of the people concerned.

ISBN-13: 978-1984365330
ISBN-10: 1984365339

Cover photo and design: Pacho Loruvacha

Also by Steph Mason

Dancing round raindrops

In memory of Esteban
My husband and true friend.
Always on my side.

Croydon, South London – December 1954

Chapter One

It was heavy. Whatever was on my feet was exceedingly heavy.

My breath beneath the blanket had transformed the sofa into a warm cocoon. This was my time of uninterrupted luxury. The final hour in my own bed was an agony of frozen fingers and toes, but when I heard the scrape of the poker against the grate, I knew that Mum Williams was jiggling the ash out of the old fire before tightly scrunching up a few sheets of newspaper and carefully placing four sticks of kindling under a small pile of anthracite to light warmth back into our home.

Mum Williams slept sitting upright on the far edge of the sofa under the brown blanket which now covered me. At the sound of the poker I would jump out of bed, run across the bedroom, and dash down the arctic stairs that were the no-man's-land between the shop and the living room. Taking a flying leap after I banged my way through the living room door, I would land on the sofa and snuggle my stiffened toes into the cosy cushion that had padded Mum Williams' rump throughout the night.

I had pulled the heavy blanket right over my head, and squirmed my six-year-old body up to the second cushion. My breath and the emerging fire had created a soporific heaven.

I wiggled my feet beneath the weight.

Long fingers grabbed a large handful of my hair.

Ripped off the sofa, the blanket dragging behind me, I was slammed into the wall before I had time to open my eyes. Smoke was in my face and brown stained fingernails were grappling around my neck and shoulders, flinging me back and forth.

"Kick me, would you?"

The lips spat the words in my face from between gritted teeth that held half a burning cigarette. My right ear caught on a nail sticking out of the window frame before I was pulled back again and launched into the wall, scull first.

"Daddy! I was waking up …"

He was on me again, lifting me up like a rag doll and shaking, shaking, shaking. "Think you can kick me, do you?"

A small hand appeared on his sleeve, Kath's hand. Hilda's plumper one landed on the other arm.

"Let 'er be Gerard … she's only a nipper."

The knobbly, vein covered fingers of Mum Williams were clamped across my chest, pulling me out of my father's grip and depositing me, and my swelling lip, behind her.

"You sit down there Gerard and Kath 'ull get you a nice cup o' tea. Don't you worry 'bout nuffink ..."

"She shouldn't be kicking her father, when her Mother's in the hospital. She needs some respect and some sense knocking into her."

"Well she's 'ad that now, 'an there's no need to go upsetting yerself no more. 'ilda get a sixpence from the tin and take Margy down the road while Gerard 'as a quiet sit down with 'is tea."

My sister, Christine, toddled into the living room with a face looking like the start of a wail. Mum William's arthritic knees almost galloped past me, sweeping the one-year-old into her arms before commanding Hilda to "Get 'er down the road ...

"Now young madam, let's get that night-time nappy off before yous start ballin' the 'ouse down as well! Where's that tea Kath?" Mum Williams bellowed as she disappeared into the kitchen while Hilda wrapped a coat around me, plonked a hat on my head and encased my shaking hands in a pair of woolly mitts.

"Shushup now Margy, shushup," Hilda said, pushing me out of the door into the yard that was still crisp with the night's frost. "It won't 'urt you much. We'll put a cold flannel on it when we gets back. Shushup now Margy!" Her apron was scrubbing away at my plump cheeks, wiping my tears. She sucked at the edge of the fabric and used it to rub a streak of blood from my lip. Then she sucked it again to stop the blood from staining her apron. "You shush and we'll go get a quarter from the corner shop." She grabbed my hand firmly and paraded me out of the front gate into the spotlight of the neighbours.

"Is the li'l one all right 'ilda," Mrs Phillips was waddling to catch up with the latest gossip, "What 'appened to 'er then?" she challenged directly she drew level and could see my thick lip and red eyes.

"Gerard 'ad a go at 'er," Hilda confided in a stage whisper behind her hand. "Poor lil bitch, 'e's all worked up wiv Flora's 'ealth and the noo baby. She didn't do nuffin' wrong really, but 'e went for 'er like nuffin' you've never seen."

"All right there Margy?" Mrs Philips coo-ed as she gave a brutal squeeze to my bruised cheek. "Don't you worry, you're goin' to get a beautiful new sister so I 'eard, so that's somefing to smile about if ever I 'eard one!" and she gathered herself across the street, leaving us to the mercy of half a dozen other locals in whom Hilda confided the spice of the morning's events before we arrived at Mr and Mrs Liptons shop.

The grocery was fronted by barrels full of broken biscuits – I would spend ages trying to find whole biscuits in those barrels. To discover one was a prize worth all the searching. I loved the smell of that shop. The thick, knotty floorboards squeaked at the entrance, making the bell above the door redundant. The walls were lined with round bins, the same size as me, containing flour, rice and sugar. Large cheeses and hams sat beneath polished glass domes, while spices, sultanas, tea and cocoa powder lived in labelled drawers beneath the wooden counter. The boiled sweets in their tall glass jars gave a splash of colour across the back wall. Stripy humbugs, chocolate limes, lemon drops, long sticks of pink and white rock, little packets of violets … what was my rude awakening worth?

I went for chocolate limes. After they had been carefully weighed out into the white paper bag on the gently swaying copper scales, Mr Lipton popped a lemon drop into my mouth and ruffled my hair.

Hilda had whispered all the details of my father's morning fury to the rest of the staff and customers, leaving no part of the action unembellished, and we left the shop to a purred chorus of "… poor li'l bitch … shame … 'E's not free with 'is fists as a rule … just in a tizz about the misses … she'll be alright wiv Mrs. Williams …"

Mrs Williams, or Mum Williams to me, had been widowed a decade earlier. She had four daughters of her own. The eldest was Kath – who had effectively stepped into her father's shoes as the head of the family. Then there was Hilda, Marjory and Ivy. Before Ivy was born, Mum Williams and her husband, Albert, had also adopted my mother, Flora.

By the time we arrived home the living room was full of the smell of bacon and eggs. Philip was sitting up at the table, his breakfast encased between two pieces of bread.

"Get a move on Margy or you'll be late for school."

"Am I going today?" I asked, looking up at Mum Williams. "I thought we were going to collect the baby."

"Not til you get back this afternoon, I've a load of things to do this mornin'. Kath'll take us up t'Mayday at three."

My father was sitting on the sofa nursing a cup of tea, a cigarette and a scowl.

"Are you going to go see about the noo 'ouse Gerard?" Hilda asked him cautiously. "They'll probably give you somefink ever so grand wiv 'free children an' an ill wife."

"Flora said she would hold out for one of the big corner ones on the new estate, if the baby didn't kill her before she got there …" he muttered.

My father's Irish accent was soft, he had a mellow voice, as a rule, and was particular about how he spoke. Although he was skinny, he had the reputation of a charmer and loved making people laugh. I looked up at him. Was my mother going to die? I was pondering what that would feel like when Mum Williams piped up.

"Get yerselves down the road, the pair of you."

The doctors had found a shadow on my mother's lung. She and my father had been living in a damp basement flat and the pea-souper fogs of the late 1940s and early 1950s had already led to millions of people developing deadly bronchitis and pneumonia. TB remained a killer, although less so since penicillin came on the scene. The Clean Air Act was still two years away and the winter smogs, created by a mixture of fog and smoke from all the household fires, were in full flow in December 1954. Any chest infection was a serious matter, especially in a woman who had just given birth, so my father was understandably concerned.

By the time I became an adult I had grown a healthy disregard for the number of ailments that were imminently going to despatch my mother to the other world, but at the age of six the notion seemed slightly more interesting.

As Philip and I grabbed our satchels and raced for the door, Mum Williams began her after-meal walk, slowly back and forth from the table in the living room through to the kitchen, clearing the breakfast dishes into a shallow stone sink. She had probably suffered from rickets as a child as her legs were so bowed that the shins protruding from beneath her skirt made a perfect half circle.

Her dress never varied; a muddy coloured skirt and jumper would be covered with a clean flowery pinny that crossed over at the back protecting everything except her sleeves. Her legs were encased in thick opaque tan stockings which ended in big tartan slippers that came up around her ankles. The slippers had a bobble on the top and thick soles underneath. Her long grey hair reached below her waist but was always done up in a bun, pinned to the nape of her neck. She had broken her nose in the accident that killed her husband five years before I was born. The crooked nose on one side was matched by a spreading birthmark on the other side of her face beneath her right eye. She never wore make-up or glasses. Mum Williams was already sixty-six and suffered horribly from arthritis. She was very tiny and very old fashioned, and I adored her.

Philip was the son of Kath's best friend, Violet. He was six years older than me and had started at the secondary school just across the road. I had to go about half a mile further to Howard Primary, and Hilda was soon puffing behind me to catch up and take my hand. Every morning she would walk me to the gates in a respectable manner before setting off on the round of daily chores Mum Williams had ordained she needed to do before she went to work herself. Today was Wednesday, early closing day, so Hilda was only working a half-day at the florist and would be home before we even got out of school. We were going to have a perfect afternoon.

****

Mum Williams was still busy in the coal shop when I ran through the front gate.

"Give us an 'and in 'ere Margy," she called out as she heaved a bag of anthracite from the pile. "Anything else Mr Moseley?" she enquired. "Margy, can you weigh them bundles of kindling for Mrs Nightingale …"

I liked helping in the shop. Often we weren't very busy which was why Mum Williams also kept her sewing machine in there. Nobody was ever idle in our household, there was always some money-making scheme going on, but today I wanted to get rid of the customers as quickly as possible, bolt down our cup of tea and head off for the hospital. Marjory was coming over to take care of my sister, Christine, while Kath, Hilda, Mum Williams and I went to collect my new baby sister. I was in a fever of excitement.

It seemed to take an age for the teapot to be washed, the boat-shaped baby bottles to be put in to soak ready for the new arrival, and for Mum Williams to finally remove her pinny.

Hilda went upstairs to change while Mum Williams stood in front of the only mirror in the house, above the mantelpiece in the living room. She took a comb from the shelf and ensured the few vagrant hairs that had dared to escape her bun were put back in place before she extracted an evil-looking spike from her enormous hat and used it to pin the crown securely to her scalp. Even in a gale Mum Williams' hat never moved from her head. With the addition of her gabardine coat, we were, at last, out of the door.

Kath was the family's driver. Always dressed in trousers, Kath had been the son her father never had. From an early age she had helped in the family's coal business and when young men were in short supply during the Second World War, Kath drove the delivery van and was responsible for keeping many families warm throughout the Croydon district. She always drove a big car. The current one had running boards, doors that opened the wrong way, no seat belts and a small rack on the back above the boot handle. This usually housed our picnic things because Mum Williams worried it might be dangerous for children to sit out there if we went round steep corners. However, if there were too many of us, a couple of kids would ride up on the rack, hanging on for dear life.

Mum Williams gently lowered herself into the front seat as Kath took hold of the massive steering wheel and jiggled the long gearstick into position. Hilda was holding open the big double gates as I stretched my neck to see out of the window and wave at the boys from my school who were playing football in the street.

Hilda jumped in as Kath tooted her horn to shoo the kids out of the way, and we were off.

"What was it like when I was born?" I asked hoping they would humour me with a full rendition of my arrival.

"Ooo Margy, you was absolootly bootiful," Hilda began.

"You took an 'ell of a long time to get 'ere, caused 'alf the road to go deaf with the squealing, an' cost a small fortune, as I remember it," Kath put in caustically.

"You was breech," Mum Williams explained, "that's why we 'ad to get the doctor in the end an' 'e charged seven an' six."

"You can get a dog licence for less than that," Kath said, "but it were worth it cos it stopped the squealing, although we were eatin' potato stew for two weeks afterwards to pay for you. Philip 'ad us roaring though, 'e took one look an' said 'What's that?', 'It's a little girl' Mum says, 'I don't want it, send it back!' 'e says. Ooo we did laugh at that!"

"Yer Mum did squeal summut rotten," Hilda agreed. "Kath were shouting up the stairs 'Can't you shut 'er up Mum, we'll 'ave all the neighbours knockin' on the door.' But it didn't do no good. Squealed so loud you could 'ear 'er at the Blackwall Tunnel, that's 'ow we knowed you was born just after midnight, cos the squealin' stopped."

I had been born two months after the National Health Service got underway, at a time when almost all women gave birth at home. Hospitals were viewed with fear and suspicion, something which Mum Williams and Hilda never got over. However, both my sisters were delivered in NHS institutions that now provided wonderful free care for everyone.

The Mayday Hospital was only three miles away from our home at 21A West Street. There was a special entrance for the Maternity Ward and Kath's great vehicle was soon sweeping through the grounds before stopping to the left of some wide stone steps. Hilda and Mum Williams got out of the car. As they made their way up the steps a nurse emerged from the doorway with a well-wrapped bundle in her arms. She was followed by my parents. There was a short conversation, none of which I could hear because it was a cold December day and the windows of the car were firmly shut. A couple of minutes later the nurse handed the bundle to Hilda while my parents walked briskly down the steps and off to the right. They didn't stop or wave.

Mum Williams' creaky knees began crabbing their way back towards us in the car, while Hilda followed, her face flushed with awe, looking as if she were carrying the crown jewels.

"Can I see her? Please can I see her," I cried as soon as Hilda had wiggled her way into the back seat.

"Ahh Margy aint she lovely, aint she just a peach, oh Mum look at 'er, aint she lovely," Hilda cooed.

"It's not right, yer know," Kath growled.

"She's called Martina," Mum Williams announced. "Reckon they were 'oping for a boy and 'ave just stuck an "A" on the end!"

"Mebee they'd 'ave cared for a boy," Kath put in, but any foreboding went over my head as I was desperate to be allowed to hold my new tiny sister.

"All right Margy, you can 'old the body and I'll 'old the 'ead, 'ow's that? Ooo ain't she a peach! Drive quick Kath we need to get 'er in front of a good fire."

****

Winter darkness had taken hold by the time we got back to 21A. We shivered our way through the front door groping for the light switch. Kath headed straight for the stove.

"Ooo yes, you get the kettle on Kath, I'll bank up the fire, it's freezin' in 'ere."

Hilda was rocking the baby as Mum Williams placed the bassinet as close to the grate as she dared.

"Pop 'er in 'ilda an' go an' find some biscuits to go with our tea, they'll all be round for a look-see soon."

Like my mother, Mum Williams had only been blessed with daughters but they had formed a tight knit family, which was where the main difference with my family lay. Kath was the eldest daughter, followed by Hilda, Marjory and Ivy. There had been another daughter, Mabel, but she had died in infancy and my mother, Flora, had been taken in at roughly the same time. Only Kath and Hilda still lived at 21A but the other sisters were only a stone's throw away and everyone still gathered at our house every Friday night. Except for my parents.

Marjory must have heard the car arrive back from the hospital. Her house was only two down from 21A so she came over with Christine in a matter of minutes. I took Christine's hand and guided her to the wicker baby basket.

"This is our new sister, isn't she lovely! She's called Martina."

Christine looked down at the wrinkled face with a serious expression. A bald head stuck out from beneath the clean white blankets. She stared for a moment longer, then nodded and toddled off with her bulky terry nappy bouncing behind her.

Soon the living room was full of towering adults peeking down at the baby. Ivy and her husband, Uncle Cliff, had come straight from work. Philip's Mum, Violet, was chatting with Kath. Violet and Kath were life-long best friends. Unlike Kath, however, Violet wore pretty crêpe de Chine blouses, high heels and pencil skirts which I thought were wonderfully exotic. Uncle Charlie was giving Marjory a squeeze and teasing her, from the look on her face. The house was bursting with noise, laughter and endless cups of tea. It filled my chest with a happiness I could hardly contain. Adult eyes looked down on me with lashings of affection so that I never missed the hugs and kisses that might have been part of a less Victorian upbringing, I knew this family loved me, and I loved them.

****

Mum Williams had been born Nell Nichols back in 1889 in the village of Plumstead. Like many girls from poor backgrounds she had gone into service in her teens and had been forced to leave directly she fell pregnant with Kath in 1920. Nell married Albert Williams, a coalman six years younger than herself. Kath's birth was swiftly followed by Hilda's, Marjory's, Mabel's and finally Ivy's.

It had been a happy marriage and when Albert was killed Nell never went to bed again.

Their bedroom had been above the coal shop. The room became a shrine for all the things that were most precious to Nell; the picture rails were full of framed photographs, the surfaces crammed with cups won at school, cherished china dolls and every type of lifetime memento. Every corner of the room was stuffed with cabinets displaying family treasures, all of which were regularly dusted. A pump organ with ivory stops stood behind the door and there was a heavy red chenille cloth covering the table with matching curtains framing the red aspidistra that stood on the windowsill, but there was no bed and nowhere to sit down.

Since Albert's death Nell only went upstairs to fetch a change of clothes out of one of the other bedrooms. She slept sitting up on the living room sofa, while Hilda slept in the armchair next to her.

****

The party atmosphere was in full swing when a cry went up in the kitchen, "Auntie Vi's coming ..."

"Ooo bugger it! 'ide the baby," Mum Williams commanded, her face flushing red as she pulled the bassinet away from the fire. A dozen eager hands grabbed me and my sisters, the quickest ones were up the stairs and into Kath's bedroom taking Martina with them. Hilda had Christine halfway into the hallway by the time Auntie Vi stormed through the back door looking like a cross between a sergeant major and a dried up prune.

"Where is it then? Where is it?" she cried, doing a great impression of a Rottweiler on a mission.

"What are you talkin' about?" Nell soothed. "What's the matter with you Vi? 'ave a cup o' tea an' take the weight off your feet." But Nell's sister had no intention of calming down or being diverted from her quest.

"You've taken it! I know you've taken another one! Don't play dumb with me Nell Nichols! You've got another of your waifs and strays!"

There was a huge row taking place above my head, but down at my level I was trying to work out how Auntie Vi knew we had a new baby, but more than anything I was digesting the phrase "*waifs and strays*".

It dawned on me that she was referring to me and my sisters, my beautiful sisters. This was our home, but for the first time ever someone had said something which made me feel as if I didn't belong here, as if these people were not my family.

Shocked and unhappy, the maelstrom of raised voices whipped around my blonde curls, gaining in strength with every new accusation. Auntie Vi's son, Ernie, was younger than Kath, but he was a man, so when he joined in the argument it became far more serious. Warming his backside in front of the fire I heard him lecture Mum Williams as if she were a naughty schoolgirl. Hilda was crying, Marjory's voice was shrilling above Auntie Vi's while Mum Williams hung her grey head and asked if everyone wouldn't just sit down and have a slice of victoria sponge, "I done it all nice this morning, wiv strawberry jam an all ..."

"*Waifs and strays*", how could that apply to us? They all loved me. I had nice dresses to go to parties, best shoes to wear to Sunday school, good food on the table, trips to the cinema; there wasn't another kid on the street who was better cared for than me. How could I be a labelled a "waif and stray"?

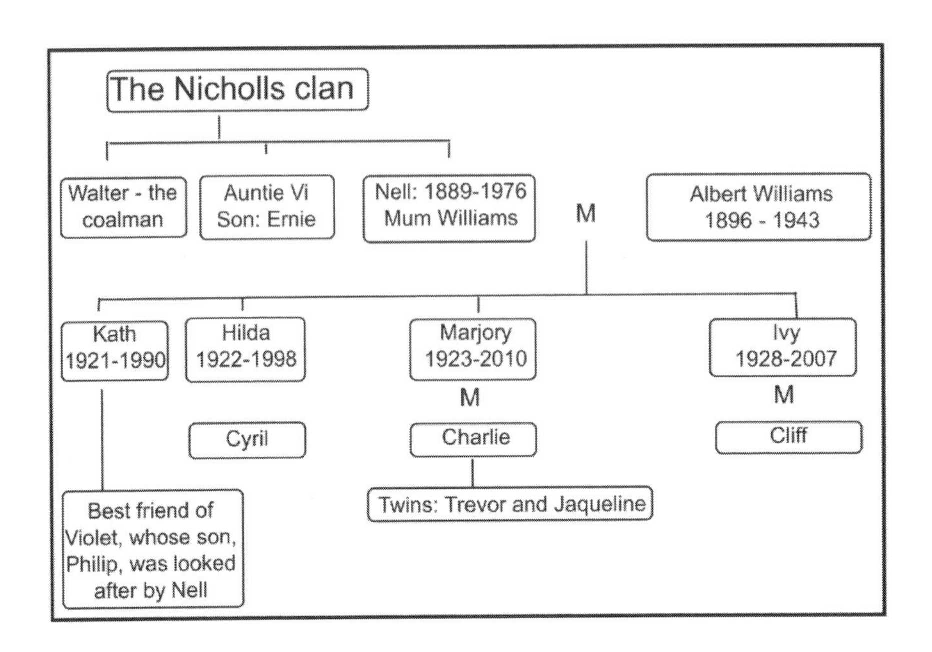
The Nicholls clan
Walter - the coalman
Auntie Vi Son: Ernie
Nell: 1889-1976 Mum Williams
M
Albert Williams 1896 - 1943
Kath 1921-1990
Hilda 1922-1998
Marjory 1923-2010
Ivy 1928-2007
M
M
Cyril
Charlie
Cliff
Twins: Trevor and Jaqueline
Best friend of Violet, whose son, Philip, was looked after by Nell

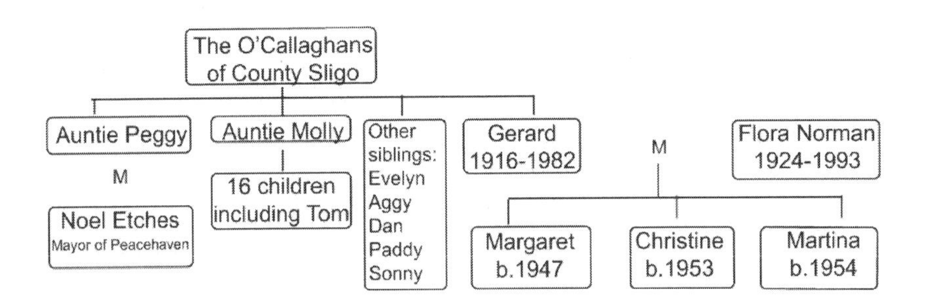
The O'Callaghans of County Sligo
Auntie Peggy
Auntie Molly
Other siblings: Evelyn Aggy Dan Paddy Sonny
Gerard 1916-1982
M
Flora Norman 1924-1993
M
Noel Etches
Mayor of Peacehaven
16 children including Tom
Margaret b.1947
Christine b.1953
Martina b.1954

Chapter Two

My mother was born in March 1924 to Irish parents who lived in the cottages opposite 21A. Christened Flora Norman, she had a sister called Winifred who was six years older than her. At the end of 1925 Flora's mother died in childbirth leaving her father, Ted, in a quandary as to what to do next.

Nell was nursing her infant daughter, Mabel, when there was a knock. Albert opened the door to find his widowed neighbour on the step.

"'Ows yerself Ted? Won't you step in for a cup o' tea?"

The whole community was rallying round Ted and his girls with pots of stew and a helping hand whenever they could manage. That was the way things were, but it was still hard on a man to bring up two young daughters when he needed to go out to work and make a living.

"What are your plans Ted?" Albert asked, anticipating an answer than involved either returning to family in Ireland or for an unwed sister or cousin to come to Croydon to take care of the children.

"The oldest one will go to the orphanage, and the baby can go to the bottom of the river for all I care …"

"You surely don't mean that Ted …" Albert replied, attempting to keep the shock out of his voice.

"I surely do! What else is a man to do? I'm taking Winifred to the nuns tomorrow, I'd take Flora with 'er but they won't take 'em under five, so I'll have to leave 'er someplace else. I've got enough to worry about without kids."

Albert looked over at Nell.

"While I'm nursin' one baby, I might as well be lookin' after two," she said quietly, "but I'm sure you'll be wantin' 'er back as soon as you're on your feet again …"

"That I won't. I'll go get 'er now."

Ted never returned to collect either of his daughters, or even to pay a visit, although he moved just three roads away from West Street. Nobody knows what happened to Winifred. Albert met Ted for a pint in 1927 to ask if he and Nell could formally adopt Flora, "just to make it right like". Ted signed the papers with the happy sigh of a burden shifted for good.

Nell and Albert didn't tell Flora she wasn't one of their own. Mabel had died shortly after Flora was taken in and the pretty toddler had served as something for the couple to focus on in their grief. When Ivy arrived the family of seven continued in the same way they always had done, everyone was treated equally, a child was a child, to be loved irrespective of its genetic heritage. If Flora had been very perceptive she might have noticed that her blonde wavy hair was rather different to that of any of her "sisters" or "parents". But she wasn't the pensive type and instead flaunted the notion round school that she was her "father's" favourite, "cos I'm the prettiest!"

When do you tell a child she's not cut from the same cloth as all the other children in the household? Flora couldn't remember her birth parents and daily life continued as usual with Albert and Nell's brother, Walter, walking over Duppas Hill every morning to the coal wharf beside the railway track that ran through Croydon towards Eastborne. Here the stately shire horses would stand patiently steaming in the chill dawn air as the men hitched up the heavy coal wagons and began their delivery rounds. Even with five daughters in the house, Nell worked alongside the men and there was once an article in the Croydon Advertiser about her being the only woman working at delivering coal before World War Two.

Eventually horse power gave way to a truck, but the lifestyle changes remained gracefully slow. Like most families the Williams's kept chickens, turkeys and rabbits to sell or supplement their diet. There was even a goat that was quite pliable towards everyone, except Flora, whom it chased.

"Think you're so pretty!" Marjory cried gleefully, "but the goat still doesn't like you."

Yet this was merely sibling rivalry, rather than evidence that my mother was treated differently, or discriminated against in some way.

The war-to-end-all-wars failed to do so, and when Kath was 18 a fresh world war broke out. Albert had seen how the 1914 war stripped the land of men, so the first thing he did was teach his daughter how to drive. If he and Walter were called up, the family business needed to survive until they got home again.

Kath's best friend, Violet, also learnt to drive. She became an ambulance driver, working all hours of the day and night as England was blitzed by German bombs. During the war years Violet married and in 1941 she gave birth to a son, Philip.

"Don't you worry luv, just drop 'im round 'ere when you 'av to work, I'll mind 'im," Nell said. There wasn't a baby in Croydon she wouldn't have given the same response to.

When Kath wasn't needed on the coal wagon she danced to the time-keeping tune of the factory whistle, along with Marjory and Flora. All three of the girls worked at Bourgeois Make Up factory which was close to Croydon airport – a favourite target for Hitler's Luftwaffe.

"I'm not 'aving no-one of this family dyin' without the rest of us," Nell ordered. "When that siren goes off you girls come straight 'ome. No buggering around in them shelters, you get on your bikes and pedal for all you're werf."

There was no arguing with Mum Williams once she had decreed something, so wherever they were all five girls dashed for West Street as the first warning notes began their crescendo into a full blown wail. The family stuck together through thick, thin, and German bombing raids.

On an icy Sunday night in October 1943 Kath and her parents were out making an unscheduled coal delivery. They weren't the sort who could leave folk cold if the message came through that a family had run out of fuel. Coal might be in short supply during the war years but the Williams's would always find a few shovel-fulls for anyone in need, even if it came from their own hearth. They were on their way back home. Kath dropped a gear as she approached the crossroads between Black Horse Lane and Tavern Road. A heavy rescue lorry came hurtling down the hill, slamming into the coal van with such force that it turned over. Nell went through the windscreen and woke up in hospital.

"I want t'see Albert, I want t'see my 'usband."

The nurse looked down at Nell's smashed, pleading face, "Well, you can see him love, but he's in the morgue."

Although witnesses to the crash agreed the lorry had been going far faster than it should have done and had not sounded its horn, the man at the wheel had been an Air Raid Precaution driver since 1939 and the four ARP men in the back of the lorry corroborated his version that he had reduced speed and leant on his horn twice. The lorry driver claimed twenty-two year old Kath had shot out in front of him and he had no way of avoiding her. The court found it hard to decide what was fact, and what fiction. How would it look for the war effort if the magistrates deemed five ARP men were outright liars? Kath was found guilty of driving without due care and attention and fined three pounds, but the lorry driver was found guilty of dangerous driving and fined five pounds.

At a stroke, Kath became the family's sole driver, just as Albert had feared she would; only now there was no Albert to return from the war to take over again. Kath became the man of the house, but Nell was still the matriarch and nobody was going to blame her Kath for what had happened.

"It's not right. We was there. We know, even if them magistrates don't. It won't be spoken of again," and so it wasn't.

Seventy years after the crash happened a newspaper clipping was discovered inside a family bible which told of what had transpired in court under the headline: "Father killed in collision, daughter summoned for dangerous driving". Until that point I had always thought Albert had been driving the van that night.

Kath took on the mantle of head of the household. She drove. She worked. She kept herself to herself and never murmured a word about her sad burden. Thank goodness she had her friend Violet outside of the family to talk to. Mum Williams removed the marital bed from her room and slept the next thirty-three years sitting upright on the sofa in the living room. Hilda, Nell's second daughter, kept her mother company by bedding down on the brown leather chair that slid backwards and had a footrest that came out underneath it. The other four girls remained upstairs as the war wound on to its conclusion.

Stiff upper lip, many families had lost far more, it wouldn't do to complain, but Kath and Nell now had a bond that bound them far tighter than any of the others. Whatever Nell wanted, Kath would back her, but if Kath needed a champion her mother would always be by her side. Nell protected Kath with a fierceness that lasted throughout the rest of her life.

****

By the time the war ended and the men were demobbed Kath, Marjory and Flora had started working at the Sleepeasy factory while Hilda worked at a local florist. As had happened after the First World War, England had a shortage of young men. The factory was a stone's throw away from 21A and it's gaggle of women, so when a new male face arrived at Sleepeasy it attracted some attention. John Gerard O'Callaghan might have been a bit skinny but he was still male. He didn't drink too much and hadn't been damaged physically or mentally by his experiences in the trenches. He was a catch.

Gerry, as he was known to all his friends, had been born in Sligo – where Mountbatten was subsequently blown up by the IRA. He was in his early thirties. His wife had been killed in the blitz whilst he was at the front, and his brother had also died. His sisters Peggy and Molly drifted over to England but the two of them retained far stronger Irish accents than the softly spoken Gerard. As well as never being without a cigarette, Gerard was never without a joke. Childlike, pretty blonde, Flora was quickly smitten by the older man who spent every break time trying to get her to laugh.

Nell was not amused. She had brought up a household of good girls. There was no scandal or disrespect for any of the Williams family and, in her opinion, Flora's relationship was progressing far too fast for a girl who was only just 21.

"But that's just it, Mum! I am 21 and I am going to marry Gerard whether you like it or not. You have to give me my birth certificate so we can take it to the registry."

"Gaw blimey! I don't 'ave no stifficut and there's no need for you to go runnin' off gettin' one. Stifficut or no stifficut you're stayin' in this 'ouse with the rest of us until a nice local lad your own age comes along, proper like. Your farver wouldn't like this, not at all 'e wouldn't."

But the arguments fell on deaf ears. Flora took herself off to lodge with Gerard's sister, Peggy, and her husband Noel. She then procured her birth certificate which informed her she was adopted. She took it down to the registry office as quickly as she could. By August 1946 she was Mrs. Gerard O'Callaghan, living in a basement flat in Coombe Road within easy walking distance of Mum Williams and, ironically, even closer to her birth father than she had been before. "Old Ted" continued with his new life and family. He passed the time of day if he saw Mum Williams, but never concerned himself with his daughter again.

As Gerard was a Catholic it didn't take long for me to show up. By September 1947 my mother had given birth, and abandoned, the first of her three daughters.

Mum Williams was sixty and already battling arthritis, but she scooped me up and started boiling nappies and making bottles without a second thought.

Although Flora cannot have known how she would feel about her first child, she had made no provision for me, knitted no booties, put no crib in her pristine basement flat. When the pains started she made her way to 21A West Street and when it was over and she had enjoyed a bit of a rest and some TLC from the only mother she could remember, she climbed back into her high heels and seamed stockings and went home to Gerard. Alone.

I was born into a house of women and they were delighted with their first "grandchild", their own living doll could not have been more loved.

Chapter three

21A West Street was a typical Croydon business-house. The coal shop was slightly recessed back from the front garden, with the door for customers to use just off the hard standing. Our own front door led into a passage. There was a door on the right leading into the shop, and on the left was another door into our front room, these two doors were flanked by interior windows, each covered in sticky wax paper to give a frosted effect so that we could see what was happening in the shop without losing too much of our own privacy.

The passage from the front door led straight up the stairs to the bedrooms. Mum Williams' roomful of treasures spread across the whole of the area above the shop. Along the landing there was the first bedroom where Kath slept in the corner double bed, while I slept in the double by the window. Kath didn't particularly like sharing her room with a small child so, periodically, I would be despatched to the back bedroom where Marjory and Ivy slept, to top-and-tail with Ivy – my favourite of all the sisters. Although we had the kitchen range and a fireplace in the front room, the bedrooms were freezing cold in winter, so the sisters would pile old coats onto the beds to try to keep out the worst of the chill. I had been born in the back bedroom which was huge and had a step down into it. The back bedroom covered the whole of the kitchen, scullery and outside toilet.

Downstairs there was the front room, which was where we spent most of our time because it was warm. The best way to describe the front room is "brown". It was all browns. The old, brown radio up on a brown shelf. A dark lino covered the floor, topped by an enormous rug that had once had a typical red pattern of the era on it. The rug had seen better days, it was stained and worn and generally brown. There was a brown sofa and Hilda's brown leather chair situated either side of the fireplace. Opposite the blackened grate there was a window flanked by brown curtains with a sideboard in front which housed a tiny black and white television set. The large wooden table was surrounded by brown wooden chairs that were used to support a stout plank either side so that a crowd of people could sit up and eat. Kath had her own chair at the head of the table and Mum Williams sat at the other end.

When we were squinting at the television we would all squash onto the sofa or Hilda's chair and draw the curtains to keep out any chink of light. At the back of the front room were the stairs that led down to the cellar.

I hated the cellar. The walls were covered in coal dust. A shoot led down from the hard standing outside and tons of coal would hurtle down to create a black mountain. It was dingy and hung with large webs which left me imagining massive spiders, camouflaged in the blackness, and ready to drop on my head. On icy days our turkeys would be kept down there and if Kath put me in the cellar as a punishment I would cling to the highest step to try and avoid their horrible beaks and vicious claws.

Kath was the family's disciplinarian. If my crime wasn't bad enough to warrant the cellar, then she would shut me in the scullery. I remember being locked in the scullery for things like picking the paint off the inside of the bedroom door. It had seemed like an important experiment to see how large a single bit I could remove, but Kath didn't see it that way. Mum Williams' toughest punishment was to say "You're a naughty girl, you're very naughty!", but Kath was more proactive.

"She's been naughty Mum, bung 'er in the scullery!" Mum Williams wouldn't like it but she always bowed to Kath's will.

The front room led into the kitchen which was large with a range and a broad stone sink in which we all washed. The scullery was at the back of the kitchen with the only entrance behind the kitchen table. Kath would shut the door leaving me in complete darkness and then I would hear the table being dragged across to act as an impenetrable lock. The scullery had racks for pots and pans plus shelves for the part that was used as a larder.

While the rest of the family spent most of their life in the front room, Kath haunted the kitchen. I don't know what she used to do in there as Mum Williams was the cook and washerwoman, but Kath was always banging about in there, it seemed to be her separate place.

The back door opened into the kitchen. Outside there was our loo and the yard where Kath's car sat next to the animal cages which housed the turkeys, chickens and rabbits.

Our house was opposite the church and the senior school. Flanking the school were Bowman's bakers, an off licence and a butchers. The local pub and the Sleepeasy factory were on the corner and the fire station was further down the street in Old Town, so there was a constant passing of people to watch, and Mum Williams spent hours standing at the gate talking to all her neighbours. There wasn't a piece of gossip that went unknown, although if it was considered even the tiniest bit risqué it would be relayed in whispered code behind a prim hand.

****

We needed the planks around the front room table as there always seemed to be so many people stopping to eat at West Street.

Often I would be hauled onto the table once the plates had been cleared away and they'd all be singing: "Oh, you beautiful doll, you great big beautiful doll, let me put my arms around you, I could never live without you ..." I would dance up and down the table enjoying every second of their undivided attention. When the singing had finished they would ask me to recite the story of Old Ecke Thump in a broad Yorkshire accent. They never tired of hearing about "Me old darlin' sweetheart Ecke Thump ..." and could be relied upon to laugh at the right moments every single time.

They indulged me constantly. Even when I drove Philip mad by walking over his prize train set, I would only receive the mildest reprimand. Mum Williams would despatch Hilda up to her treasure trove to retrieve my china doll and the little pram so that I could promenade up and down the street and leave Philip in peace.

Auntie Vi must have been more tolerant when I was the only toddler there, as I remember her bringing over great bundles of towels and clothes that had been left at the Turkish baths where she worked. All our towels had a line of blue around the edge with Welling Municipal Baths printed on it. The family would sit around the table and look through the goodies Auntie Vi had brought and Mum Williams would be saying, "... that'll do for Marjory, and that'll fit our Kath."

Mum William's brother, Walter, was also a regular visitor. He had gone to work for another coal merchant after Albert's death and whenever he arrived Nell would dash around on her bandy legs crying, "sit down, sit down, no Walter, wait a minute, not yet!" as she grabbed a newspaper to cover the chair. "Oh hurry up Nell!" he'd say jokingly as he pretended to plonk himself into an unprotected chair. He was always filthy, completely black from head to foot.

My parents did not visit very often. Even when an unexploded bomb was discovered in a neighbour's front garden and they were evacuated from their basement flat for a time, they didn't come to West Street. I suppose they must have gone to stay with Peggy and Noel.

Although I didn't realise it, this was an odd time. In some areas there were still horse drawn milk floats, but at the same time Mr Churchill was announcing that Britain had made an atomic bomb, making us the third nuclear power after the USA and the Soviet Union.

The month before Churchill's announcement, in February 1952, the king died and the whole country was plunged into mourning. Princess Elizabeth seemed so petite and young to be taking on the role of Queen.

In November of that year we had another big shake up, but this one was closer to home and far more personal.

Derek Bentley was a 19 year old lad who lived not far from us. He came from a good family, who were well liked in Croydon. Everyone knew Derek was a couple of sandwiches short of a picnic. He had even failed the National Service test which was hard to do! I believe when he had been born he had been normal but a bomb dropped on the family home during the war and Derek had been hit on the head and buried in the rubble which led him to suffer from epileptic fits. Although Derek's parents and sister, Iris, tried to keep him away from any undesirable influences, he ran into a 16-year-old boy from a bad family. The boy's name was Chris Craig, his brothers had already been in prison for twelve years and Chris fancied himself as a hard nut.

Chris persuaded Derek to burgle the warehouse of Barlow and Parker on the Tamworth Road on the night of November 2nd. As they climbed over the gate they were spotted by a nine year old girl who told her mother, and she swiftly phoned the police. Chris was carrying a gun that he had modified so it would fit into his pocket. He had lent Derek a knife and a knuckleduster. When they heard the sirens the pair fled to the roof of the building. Derek was caught by Detective Sergeant Frederick Fairfax. The detective allegedly said "Give me the gun, son" to Craig, at which time Derek was reported to have uttered the ambiguous phrase, "Let him have it, Chris." Craig shot Fairfax in the shoulder, but the detective kept hold of Derek who made no attempt to use his own weapons. When more police began exiting the staircase onto the roof Chris used the remainder of his ammunition on the first man out, which was PC Sidney Miles.

A policeman was killed and someone had to pay. Craig was under age so Derek was charged under the law of "joint enterprise" and, despite a plea for mercy from the jury, was sentenced to hang. All over the country there was a surge of public opinion against the verdict, but capital punishment was carried out as quickly as possible at Wandsworth Prison on the 28th of January 1953.

If much of the rest of the nation questioned the hanging of Derek Bentley, the feeling in Croydon was far more strident.

"That was wicked what they did, Derek didn't 'ave 'alf 'is marbles, everyone noo that!" Marjory ranted when Mum Williams brought the news in from the street that the execution had taken place.

"It can't be right. I'm not going to believe nothing til I sees it in the noospaper." Mum Williams said. "They're a lovely family – a bit dotty about all their pets an' all, but you can't blame folk for lovin' animals. They can't 'ave killed 'im, they just can't." But they had.

"'e was that gullible the police could 'ave got 'im to say anything, an' 'e wouldn't 'ave realised the trouble 'e was getting' 'imself into," Kath reasoned. Nobody thought it was right, and there was a lengthy outpouring of sympathy and support for the Bentley family in their quest to clear their son's name.

Around this time I began to see more of my mother. She wasn't visiting to do motherly things, although as sweets came off ration in February she did bring me a Fry's Chocolate Crème or a Five Boys chocolate bar whenever she came. That was the only thing she brought to the house, apart from her knitting. There were no expectations that I should remain in the same room when my mother visited, but as everything happened in the front room I was usually there, playing on the floor or colouring at the table when she arrived. She probably wouldn't say anything to me. There was certainly no hugging or kissing or questions about what I had been up to.

Flora would stay for an hour. She was due to give birth to my sister Christine in April but she wasn't knitting baby clothes, it was probably a cardigan for my father or some socks.

My mother was very glamorous compared to the rest of us. She would wear a black straight skirt with a sleeveless floral smock that covered her pregnant tummy. Beneath this there would be a white blouse with a Peter Pan collar, fastened with a cameo broach. Her stocking seams would be straight and her heels were always quite high. She had pretty wavy blonde hair that framed her face, but she was a cold fish although this was masked by a child-like temperament. In general the sisters admired Flora with her pristine flat, elegant clothes and older husband. Kath used to chat to Flora a great deal and was always asking her opinion on things. It didn't seem to occur to any of them that my mother was only visiting more frequently because she would soon need them to take charge of her next child.

****

Ivy was courting Cliff and Marjory was seeing Charlie. Mum Williams liked both the lads although Charlie's habit of sitting in the front room whistling and stamping his feet in time to his chosen tune led her to regularly call up the stairs, "'urry up Marjory before he wears the pattern off the lino!"

It was acceptable for the couples to go and visit people or, at a pinch, go to the cinema together. So that was where Ivy and Marjory told their mother they were going.

"Ivy and Cliff 'ave gone to visit 'is aunt, she 'asn't been well lately," Marjory would hear her mother telling the neighbours.

"Well that's odd as I saw them in the bushes at Caterham Hill," she would whisper to Kath with a wink.

"You only knows that cos you an' Charlie were in the next door bush!" Kath would whisper back with a toss of her head as she left for the kitchen.

"So, what if we was! It's a free country Kath Williams!"

With two of the sisters occupied for most of the hours when they weren't at work, the burden of caring for the new baby, Christine, once again, dropped squarely onto the shoulders of Mum Williams. She delegated extra tasks to Hilda, and another baby took up residence in Kath's room. The big copper boiler that Mum Williams used to wash nappies in was pressed back into action. Every couple of days she would be pummelling the life out of the towelling with a wooden pole and bleach to get them white as snow. Then they would be put through the mangle in the yard to get as much of the water out as possible. Everything had to be spotless. If Hilda was doing the washing and tried to cut corners, a shout would ring out of the back door, "'ilda! You can't put them on the line! Look at the state of 'em! You'll 'ave the neighbours talkin'." And the whole lot would have to be done again.

I used to hate being asked to help with the mangle. Whoever was turning the handle would make me hold the sheets or nappies tight until the very last piece of cloth was eaten by the evil rollers. I was always sure my small fingers were going to be sucked in and mangled too.

Once our clothes were dry, which could take days in the winter time, Mum Williams would remove the cloth from the front room table and cover it with blankets and an old sheet before warming her irons by the fire and putting in perfect creases. Everyone was always turned out impeccably. We wouldn't have been allowed out of the house if we didn't look clean and neat.

Later, someone bought Nell a Morphy Richards electric iron. It was yellow with a black handle, but she was so worried that it would blow the house to smithereens that she refused to use it unless someone else was nearby to rescue her if the worst happened.

Although Hilda was treated as the resident drudge, her chores weren't all washing and cleaning, she was also my daily child-minder and I would get to go everywhere and anywhere she was sent. If Mum Williams wanted jellied eels for Saturday tea the two of us would be dispatched to Tooting Broadway market on the old tram to pick out the best ones we could find among the buckets of wriggling creatures. As custom demanded, if Mum Williams thought the eels were nice and fat I would be praised to the hilt for "pickin' out a loada gooduns", while if she considered them undersized Hilda would be berated for "bein' taken for a bloody fool by them market traders." Poor Hilda!

Hilda would also take me to any medical appointments I had, or to buy the few clothes I needed, or to the Dolls Hospital if one of my toys had an "accident" in our overcrowded home.

I was never upset if one of the toys became slightly damaged as I adored the Dolls Hospital in South Croydon. Hilda would steer me gently off the bus as I cradled my injured doll, all wrapped up in a white blanket. When we arrived I would be called forward and my doll would be given a patient number, her name would also be recorded as would the name of her "mummy" – which made me feel very proud and responsible. The lady at the front desk would explain how long it would take to make my doll "better", and after this solemn conversation, we would leave with heads held high due to the importance of our mission.

At the beginning of June, six weeks after my sister Christine arrived, Princess Elizabeth was crowned Queen of England, Scotland, Wales and Northern Ireland. We rented a new nine inch television in order to watch the pomp and ceremony. It might have been black and white but we were able to imagine the splendour of the Golden Coach and the ermine trimming around all the red velvet gowns worn by the aristocrats. It rained, but that couldn't dampen anyone's spirits. While Richard Dimbleby commented for thirteen hours straight, the whole family – apart from my parents – drifted in and out of the front room in a state of complete euphoria. Everything was "bootiful", each shot of the queen was greeted with "ooo"s and "ahhh, look at 'er, ain't she lovely." Mum Williams was happily feeding everyone all day long – "Goo on, 'ave anuver one, I've done 'em all nice!"

Bunting festooned every street, and the trestle tables were piled with mountains of cup-cakes, carefully iced in red, white and blue. We were all so proud of our new queen and her handsome husband. A few days before the coronation, news came through that Edmund Hillary and Sherpa Tenzing had reached the summit of Everest on a British funded expedition, it felt as if the nation was on top of the world.

A month later the serial killer John Christie was hung at Pentonville Prison. While there were no regrets at this execution from anyone at 21A West Street, the fact that another man had been hung three years previously for two of Christie's murders certainly struck a chord.

"It ain't right. They got it wrong again! Just imagin' what 'e went through bein' accused of killin' 'is own wife and child! 'E'd already lost them an' then 'e 'ad to swing for it!"

Capital punishment was getting a bad name that year.

****

It was time for me to start school. I was nervous, but hugely excited. Mum Williams had made sure all my blue knickers had a pocket sewed into them for my handkerchief, I was scrubbed behind my ears and my garters kept my socks securely round my knees, all the sisters – except for my mother - had had a whip round for my new shoes, I was ready to go.

Kath and Marjory worked in the Sleepeasy factory and started work at 7.30, but Ivy had the brain cell of the family and was an office worker. She didn't have to leave until almost 9 o'clock to walk over Duppas Hill to her place of work, so she would often run errands to the baker and the green grocer for Mum Williams before she left.

I adored Ivy, she always had a big smile and a soft voice. She never became embroiled in the constant needling between Kath and Hilda, and she avoided being drawn into any beef Marjory had against anyone. She was calm, but fun and would always help me with my colouring or other projects. She was so frightened of thunder and lightning that at the first rumble she would hide underneath the table, but everyone still accepted that Ivy was the smart one among us.

There were some tall Edwardian houses that backed onto our property with steps in front of them and big stone balustrades before the front doors. In one of these lived a woman called Mrs Coatman. She used to throw dead pigeons into our yard. I don't know what her problem was with our family, but she was generally known as "The Pigeon Lady" because she used to allow the birds to fly into her house and if a cat came in she would hang the cat.

Mum Williams had asked Ivy to stop off at the greengrocers for a lettuce as she walked me to school. Mrs Coatman was creosoting her front door as we walked passed her raised balustrade. Somehow, the entire bucket of creosote "fell" from the wall covering me from head to foot.

The vile liquid was burning every part of my exposed flesh. I was screaming as Ivy gathered me into her arms and ran for the kitchen door. Mum Williams was throwing towels over me, trying to get the creosote off, but although she had done her best it was clear my eye was in a bad way. Mum Williams and Hilda were both terrified of hospitals but they didn't hesitate to head for Croydon General.

My eye had to come out to be cleaned. I was awake and screaming like mad. This time nobody said "Shushup Margy", there was no doubt, it was really bad. We were sent home with an eye-patch and an appointment at the May Day Eye Clinic. It was going to be a long haul.

Nell wanted to take Mrs Coatman to court because she was sure she had upended the bucket on purpose, but it never got that far and we just let it all float away. Several days later, when I finally got to school, I was given a book about the new Queen. It was a hard back with a blue cover and the Head Master had presented one to each child on the first day of term.

That autumn I caught whooping cough and, with the muscles at the back of my eye weakened already, the constant coughing made the eye turn round completely. Each long "whoop" wracked my child's body, thrusting my tongue out as I gasped for breath. I coughed to the point of making myself sick. Once again I had to be taken to see the doctor. Mum Williams would never come into the building in case the doctor saw her and wanted to do something about her legs, or any of the rest of her. So Hilda would be sent in with me, despite her own doctor phobia.

Directly we exited the door, Nell would peel herself away from the wall she was attempting to blend into and grab Hilda's arm, "what 'e say? What 'e say?

"She's got 'ooping cough Mum."

"What 'bout 'er eye? What's 'e goin' t' do 'bout that?"

"She'll 'ave to 'ave hoperations, but 'e doesn't know if they'll work."

"Gaw blimey, we can't 'ave the poor little bitch wiv one eye up the chimney and t-other in the pot forever! Did 'e give you a stifficut?"

As far as Mum Williams was concerned, having a "certificate" was the thing that showed you had seen a real doctor. It was monumentally important. All the rest of the information was just window dressing.

Chapter Four

Hilda was the only one of the sisters who worked in a shop, so she was the only one who had a half day on Wednesdays. This became our treat afternoon. When I came home from school Hilda would have combed her large, under-rolled, fringe into place while the rest of her brown hair would be curled at her shoulders. Marjory, Hilda and Ivy all used to roll their bangs against their foreheads, securing them with big silver clips every night. Deep curls were in fashion. For our outings Hilda would wear one of her smart taupe suits with a fine white pinstripe running through it, topped with padded shoulders and broad collar. Beneath her straight skirt would be sheer stockings and a white handbag would be matched with peep-toe shoes.

Hand-in-hand we would walk down to the Davis Theatre on Croydon High Street, passing the time of day with everyone we met. Even when dressed up, Hilda would ensure she didn't smile broadly because her teeth were completely rotten. She was too terrified of the dentist to get anything done about it.

The Davis Theatre showed all the latest films from Britain and America. We saw the Marx Brothers and Key Stone Cops, but in truth we didn't mind what was on, we just took pot luck on the matinee of the day. Hilda would pay eight pence for me to get in while she would go in the 1'3ds (costing one shilling and three pence, known as "the one and threes") or, if she was feeling flush, the 1'9ds. The cinema was huge with a foyer tiled in black and white diamonds and a plush round sofa in the middle. In the centre of the sofa there were aspidistras and other exotic plants while the whole building was draped from ceiling to floor in dark red velvet edged in gold.

The lady at the ticket office served us from behind an ornate golden grill. Over the years she got to know me well and she would give me chocolates at Christmas. After she presented us with our little paper tickets they would be punched by the usher. During the interval the ticket lady would walk down to the front of the theatre with a tray of cigarettes and small tubs of vanilla ice cream with little plastic spoons. We would make an orderly queue down the aisle and then try to make them last throughout the second half, although they had usually melted within minutes.

If we arrived back home after the factory workers, trouser-clad Kath never failed to put her oar in, "What you all done up like a dog's dinner for?" she'd ask Hilda with a sneer.

"Muuum!" Hilda would wail. "She's bein' 'orrid again. Stop 'er Mum, I ain't done nuffin' to 'er!"

“Now then Kath …” from Mum Williams, which would never stem Kath’s tide of contempt.

“What’s the point in puttin’ on white clothes when yer teeths all black?” she’d call out as Hilda started to snivel and moved towards the stairs to remove her finery for another week.

****

For the Christmas of 1953 there were two more people to fit on the planks around the front room table. We had been making paper-chains with glue and coloured paper for weeks to decorate the house with. Hilda had been sent up and down the stairs to retrieve the best china and the sherry glasses, and all the other bits and pieces from Mum’s room, until she didn’t know if she was on her way up or down. The smell of winter spices pervaded every room as we stuck cloves in oranges while Mum Williams baked piles of mince pies and buried thruppenny bits and little silver sixpences in the Christmas pudding. Every year the build-up was immense, but this year we would have men at our feast as Charlie was now engaged to Marjory, and Ivy betrothed to Cliff.

The turkey had to be stuffed and then hung in the oven because it was too massive to cook any other way. Suspended from the great meat hook, it would dribble out its juices while slowly cooking all night long. Christmas Eve was fraught as the turkey had to be got into the oven and the preparations finished for the rest of the feast so that on Christmas morning Mum Williams could don her new pinny and indulge in her annual glass of sherry.

Our presents would be underneath the Christmas tree. Mostly they were home-made. It was a tremendous effort to keep all the gifts secret despite the fact that we were tumbling over one another in that house. I wanted a bike. More than anything I wanted a bike. I didn’t care what it looked like so long as it had two wheels. My fascination with wheels has lasted all my life, but this was the first time I thought I might actually get some.

We began to unwrap our presents. My one looked uncomfortably small. Removing the paper I found a bell. Against my wishes, as I wanted to look brave in front of Charlie and Cliff, my eyes filled with tears.

“What’s the good of that!” Mum Williams cried, “a bloomin’ bell and no bike!”

“I don’t know what Farver Christmas is playin’ at!” one of the others chipped in.

“I guess ‘e’s that busy that sometimes ‘e gets it wrong.”

“But I wrote a letter and it definitely went up the chimney,” I said in a small sorrow-filled voice.

"Awww, shushup there Margy, you keep that bell safe and 'e'll probably bring you the bike next year."

I fished my handkerchief out from the pocket in my knickers and tried to cheer up as the banquet appeared from the kitchen.

The lucky money was found in the pudding and the dishes were cleared away and being washed in the big stone sink. Darkness had already wrapped up Croydon when Cliff and Charlie announced they were "stepping outside for a breath of air."

A few minutes later Mum Williams called me.

"Cliff's in the yard, 'e wants you ..."

I peered out of the door and saw Cliff wheeling a bike out from behind Kath's car. I had never expected to get a new one, but the boys had done a wonderful job at rubbing down the old frame and repainting it. The tyres were clean and the brake handles were shiny. Soon it would be resplendent with my brand new bell.

"Oh Mum! There's a bike out there! Do you think it's for me?"

"What? A bike? That Farver Christmas is a silly old bugger, 'e couldn't get it down the chimney so 'e 'id it! 'E could 'ave left us a note!"

****

My eyes now pointed in different directions. Many men had come back from the war with serious eye injuries so there were excellent eye clinics all over the country, and there was also one in Croydon. As I was so young the doctors initially thought it might be possible to get my eyes looking in the same direction with exercises.

I would go into the eye clinic with Hilda while Mum Williams waited outside. The building was pale green throughout and smelt strongly of disinfectant. A tall lady doctor with thick brown hair and a white coat would give me a new pink NHS eye patch and then the exercises would begin.

There was a chair that could be wound up and down in front of machines which looked like old fashioned cameras. The machines had handles on the side and I would have to look through the lens and put a lion into a cage.

"Is the lion in the cage?" the doctor would ask me.

"Yes!" I would say, with complete confidence, until I stepped back from the machine and saw that the lion was in one corner and the cage in the other. The exercises made no difference at all and the consultant, Mr Pearce, soon realised that the only way to get both eyes back in the right place would be through a succession of operations. The first of these was scheduled for when I was six and it happened at Moorfields Eye Hospital in London just after Christmas.

In the children's department at Moorfields there was a huge fish tank and lots of toys. Ivy was with me so I wasn't allowed to be frightened, but I was sad that I would miss Marjory and Charlie's wedding the following day.

"Don't you worry about that," Ivy said, squeezing my hand. "When Cliff and I get married you can be our bridesmaid to make up for it."

"Are you going to have a big white wedding in church then?"

"No silly! We're going up the registry same as everyone else, but we'll make you a pretty dress and you can stand behind us and hold my flowers and everything."

I breathed a sigh of pure bliss, infused with Dettol.

When the operation was over, Mr Pearce came and had a look under my eye patch.

"I'm very pleased with that," he said smiling down at me, "We'll do a bit more next time." It was the first of eleven eye operations. My parents were informed each time when I was going in for another one, but they weren't the type to do hospital visits let alone send a bunch of grapes.

I'm not sure how Mr Pearce could have known he was pleased with the operation as my eye looked like a lump of raspberry jelly for a considerable time after each bout of surgery. I spent a large part of my school life wearing a pink NHS eye patch with holes along the top for air and green material inside. This was more to protect other people from having to look at my bloody eye than because I needed the patch for medical reasons. Naturally I got ribbed about it and I perfected the art of making people laugh so that I could usually ensure any tormentors ended up looking rather foolish.

****

It was lucky that Marjory and Charlie got married before Ivy or there would have been even more of us piled into Kath's bedroom. Charlie found a house for the two of them in our street. It was far posher than ours. It had a bathroom. As both of them worked at the factory, Mum Williams reckoned they wouldn't have time to cook for themselves so she began cooking two of everything and popping one into Marjory's house just before they arrived home. On Fridays everybody still gathered at 21A for the evening and often on Sundays as well, so we still saw Marjory and Charlie constantly. Before they had been married five minutes Marjory's waistline began to expand noticeably and when she was six months into her pregnancy the midwife announced she could hear two heart beats. The couple were stunned.

"Twins, straight off!" Charlie cried, punching the air to show how great he thought the news was, but Marjory was more reserved. It was a daunting prospect on her first pregnancy even with Mayday hospital comfortably close.

"Don't you fret," Mum Williams would try to reassure her, "a good dose of caster oil will get those two out like a couple o' bars o' soap!"

Ivy and Cliff hadn't managed to find a place to rent so it was agreed that they would occupy the back bedroom once the knot was tied. It was early autumn and my mother had started paying us regular visits once again.

There was a new bump underneath her smock and a new piece of unidentifiable knitting. Each time she visited, Kath would share a cup of tea with Flora. The difference was striking. Kath in her slacks with her hair in rollers beneath a scarf turban would sit listening to her pristine adopted sister recount stories of rather glamorous weekends in Brighton with Peggy and Noel, but if Christine needed a nappy change or Mum Williams was having a bad day with her arthritis and sitting down at the kitchen table between her endless chores, the conversation would switch to how tired Flora was with another pregnancy so soon after Christine.

"I don't know 'ow I didn't die giving birth to you," my mother would say, in a way that made me feel wholly responsible for her discomfort. "I tell you, I'm not strong enough for this. This one will be the death of me. I'm sure of it."

I was already beginning to develop a suspicion that my mother's demise was not as close as she continually claimed. By contrast, Mum Williams lapped up every word. Staggering into the front room on her bowed legs, she would set another slice of freshly baked cake in front of Flora.

"Now Flora, you put your feet up and eat your cake to build up your strength. Look, I've done it all nice with icing sugar and all, just 'ow you like it."

"Oh Mum I've had a slice already!" she would say, the new piece on the way to her mouth before the end of the sentence.

"You're that skinny that when the baby's come there'll be nothin' left of you!" Mum Williams would reply, "and Gerard will be forcin' you to eat Wate-On to fill you out a bit."

How fashions have changed! Back then the ideal female form was curvy. Wate-On promised women gains of up to 30 pounds. Hoardings advertised a product that claimed it would deliver a "firm, rounded figure" filling out "the curves of bust, arms, hips and legs."

My mind wasn't on my mother. On Saturday morning I was going into town with Ivy and Cliff to buy things for their wedding and I couldn't wait.

In the end Ivy and Cliff had decided to go the whole hog and buy me a dress too. It had already been taken home, wrapped in stiff tissue paper and protected by a stout cardboard box. On Saturday we headed for Woolworths. Ivy picked out a tiny white handbag with a little silver dog on it. I was sure she was going to buy it for herself, but she turned to me and said, "Let's get you this to keep your handkerchief in on the big day, we can't have you fishing around in your knickers if you need to blow your nose."

I could hardly believe this level of extravagance, but then she bought me a white lacy handkerchief to go in there as well. White buckskin shoes and frilly white ankle socks followed and I was kitted out as the perfect bridesmaid.

****

I was so intent on my role of angelic helper to the happy couple that I had already taken the decision that, for once, I would not make Hilda run round the streets to catch me on Thursday afternoon.

Thursdays was the time when the tin bath was brought up from the cellar each week and placed in front of the fire. Great pans of water would be poured into it until the level was just about at an adult's hips.

Everyone was very respectful of others' privacy in our house. Nobody would come into the front room while bathing was in progress. Kath, however, was so private she would have her bath later, in the cellar. For the rest of us there was a strict order, Hilda would be first in the water, then Ivy and then, if they could catch me, it was my turn.

I hated the bath, there were no niceties and the water was pretty scummy by the time I got in. Mum Williams would be scrubbing away at every nook and cranny before lathering up my hair and dumping a bucket of water over the top of me without any warning to cover my eyes. The way she scrubbed my hair I used to think it would come off my head, but all my wriggling and complaining just made her more frustrated.

"For gawd's sake shushup Margy! You don't want to have to visit Nitty Nora, do you?"

Nitty Nora was the school nurse who used to carefully look through our hair for nits – it was rather like gorilla grooming on a monumental scale. She combed through each of the children's hair with a steel comb, carefully inspecting it at each pass through. Thankfully she never found any on me so I was spared the vinegar treatment and then being forced to stay at home until my head was clean. Still, I didn't want to risk an outbreak at Ivy's wedding, so I decided to grin and bear the bath.

… but I didn't have to.

"Come on Margy, I'm taking you down Scarbrook Road," Ivy announced on the Thursday afternoon, before her wedding.

The swimming pool was in Scarbrook Road too, but at that time, so were the public baths. This was posh. We were going to pay for a bath. We crossed the stone floor to the row of doors and were told to go into number three. The attendant, who was doing the same job Auntie Vi did at Welling Municipal Baths, handed us a bar of Wrights Coal Tar soap and two towels before setting the hot water going from her little station outside. We stepped into the huge, square, enamel bath from a big piece of draining wood. I got in first and then let the water out and Ivy called to the attendant, "more hot in number 3 please!" before getting into clean water herself. It was unadulterated luxury! When we came out Ivy paid a penny for us each to have a drink of hot Oxo before we went home. I had never felt so squeaky clean in my life and with my new dress, socks and shoes, I knew nothing could go wrong.

****

It was lucky Ivy had bought me the little bag and handkerchief or else I would definitely have had to hitch up my skirt. I was sobbing uncontrollably.

"That's not Uncle Walter … it can't be," sniff "if it is, 'e's gonna die!"

"Whatever are you talking about Margy? For goodness sake stop it. It's a bleedin' weddin' not a funeral!" Kath ranted

"'e's white as a sheet … 'e's very ill, 'e shouldn't be 'ere, 'e should be in bed …"

"Margy! Yer daft thing! 'e's 'ad a bath! 'e weren't born black, it's only the coal dust. Just because you've never seen him clean before don't mean he don't look the same as the rest of us underneath!"

Ivy and Cliff's wedding was a wonderful day and I don't remember missing my mother, who was "too pregnant to be present", as she put it. Marjory was also missing as she had just given birth to her twins, Trevor and Jacqueline. They were the first real grandchildren Mum Williams had.

****

A couple of months after Ivy and Cliff had moved into the back bedroom, my youngest sister Martina, arrived in Kath's room. By now Christine and I were top and tailing in the double bed under the window and the baby's cot was next to us.

It had been a big day and the content of the argument with Auntie Vi was still swimming around in my head. I pictured her small thin form, head thrust towards Mum Williams as if she were pecking her with every accusation.

“’ow many more’s she goin’ to dump on you? … Yer too old t’ be runnin’ round boilin’ bottles and nappies … Yer’ll work yerself into an early grave … ‘oo’s goin’ t’ pay for ‘em all? … ‘oo d’you think will take on all yer waifs and strays if you drop dead? … It’ll burden everyone if you makes yerself ill wiv all this … yer should have retired years ago, instead yer just takin’ on more … what are yer thinkin’ of?”

On and on it had gone with Auntie Vi marching round the front room in her sensible brogues, sensible tweed suit, sensible hairnet and Nora Batty stockings. She lectured her sister and nieces like a Sergeant Major giving his new recruits a tongue-lashing. “Children were to be seen and not heard” rather than enjoyed and cossetted. She couldn’t understand it at all, so it had to be changed. Once Ernie chimed in on his mother’s side it became far more serious. He was a man. They *had* to listen to him.

Beneath the eiderdown, with the coats piled on top of me, I felt insecure for the first time in my young life. Were the three of us really waifs and strays? Might they send us to an orphanage now that there were proper grandchildren in the family?

It occurred to me that I needed to pee. I tried not to think about it and hoped it might go away. It didn’t. The loo was awful, and twice as bad at night. I ran down the stairs and pressed my nose to the window that looked into the front room. Hilda was snoring softly. I tapped on the glass.

“Mum, I want to go to the toilet …”

“’ilda! ‘ilda!” there was no response and I could see the outline of Mum William’s leg as it shot out and kicked Hilda’s foot.

“What Mum? What? What is it?”

“Margy wants to go toilet,”

Hilda tumbled out of her chair, opening the door into the corridor where I was already shivering. “Come on then…” and she propelled me towards the kitchen and through the back door into the yard which was glistening with frost. The loo door didn’t reach the ground and I could see Hilda’s shoes and the lower part of her legs as I sat on the frozen wooden seat and groped around for the nail on which the pieces of cut up newspaper hung. Hilda was stamping her feet up and down.

“Oh hurry up, hurry up, hurry up Margy!” she hissed in a stage whisper

“I can’t find the chain!”

“Leave it, I’m freezin’ out ‘ere!”

Thawing slowly upstairs, I dropped into an uneasy sleep, blighted by images of Mum Williams not being around and having to find a way to care for my two little sisters. If we were waifs and strays, we needed to stick together.

Chapter Five

After Martina was born my mother didn't visit for a long time, although she was still working a few yards away at the Sleepeasy factory. Life rolled on as usual so I didn't notice her absence until it was announced she would be coming round for an hour one afternoon and there was a sudden flurry of extra baking and a bit of a clean-up.

Poised like royalty, my mother arrived in her beautiful patent leather court shoes and pale tan stockings. I looked up at her from the floor where I was trying to make a dolls' house out of a cardboard box. Mum Williams lumbered in with the teapot on a tray.

"Now Flora, 'ere's a nice cup o' tea. You 'ave a sit down and tell Kath all about your new 'ouse while I get Tina's feed."

"Does it 'ave a barfroom?" Kath enquired.

"Of course! It's one of the corner plots with a big garden, brand new kitchen, a bathroom and a separate toilet too."

"Indoors?"

My mother nodded as she stirred her tea.

"You was lucky to get somefin' so grand," Mum Williams called out from the kitchen where she was wiping Christine's hands after she had put them in my flour-and-water glue.

"It was cos my lungs are so weak the doctors said I need fresh air around me, and not to have no more babies. I'm too weak for any more of that. It was just the will of God that I didn't die with each one of them, especially Margaret, I'll never forget how cruel that midwife was, it's a wonder I survived!"

"You need to rest up an' get strong again," Mum Williams announced as she swapped Christine for Martina, cradling the baby on her lap and teasing the teat of the bottle into her half sleeping mouth.

"Gerard's taking me down to Brighton to visit Peggy and Noel this Sunday. They say there's nothin' so good for an invalid as sea air."

"I'd like to meet Auntie Peggy and Uncle Noel," I said tentatively from the floor, "I'd like to go to the seaside too, and I'd like to see the house you live in."

My mother looked vague, "I don't know why you'd want to see *our* house, it's very tidy and not really suitable for children ..."

"I'd still like to meet Auntie Peggy and Uncle Noel, you like them so much and they sound so nice, couldn't I come too?"

"We leave very early so we can have the whole day there and I don't think you would be ready in time."

"I can get myself up and be ready even if it's the middle of the night!"

"Aww 'ear 'er, what a big girl! She's a tribute to you Flora, she really is, it would be luverly to meet yer Auntie 'n' Uncle wouldn't it Margy!"

"Oh yes, I'd be ever so good so they liked me!"

"I'll 'ave to ask Gerard …"

"'e can't say "no" to 'is daughter meeting 'er kith and kin now she's nearly eight can 'e? She's bin taught 'er pleases and thank yous. What time do you usually leave?"

"Gerard likes to get on the road by about seven."

"That's easy then, it's even light by that time nowadays."

"Can I come then?"

"Yes, yes, I suppose so, but you've got to be ready early."

Everything I had heard about Peggy and Noel was exotic. They were always going to fancy parties and evenings with someone called The Masons, I imagined my aunt continually dressed in jewels and long dresses with huge hairstyles, while my uncle was suave with Brylcreamed hair and a black bow tie. Would they like me?

****

As usual my mother left after an hour and it was time to have dinner before Dixon of Dock Green came on our nine inch, black and white, television.

"What's for dinner?" I asked within earshot of Kath.

"Bread an' dripping! Why d'you want to know? When you get it, you'll see what's for dinner!" she replied, striding into the kitchen and banging around with the pans and plates.

I helped Christine up on to the plank and hoped she didn't say anything to set Kath off again. Christine was a fussy eater which wasn't something that went down well in our household. In the end it was me who infuriated Kath first. I watched her take a small bottle off the table and put a spoonful of its contents on the side of her plate.

"Watcha lookin' at my food for? You know that's rude. You won't be rude at table if you want t' eat!"

"Sorry Kath, I didn't mean to look at your plate, I just wondered what you put on the side …"

I should have been warned by the sly smile that came over Kath's face, "'Ere, open your mouth then and try some," she said taking a heaped teaspoon of mustard and dumping the whole lot inside my mouth.

While I was getting rid of the foul taste, Christine had decided it was time to take advantage of the mayhem.

"Don't want greens …" she said, wriggling down from the plank and beginning to run off.

"You're a naughty girl," Mum Williams said as she plonked her back in front of her plate. "I've done it all nice wiv the gravy, so you eat it up. Paper Jack wouldn't turn 'is nose up at a nice dinner like that …"

Paper Jack was well known throughout Croydon. All his clothes were made of paper which was kept up with string and rubber bands. Mum Williams would often give him a cup of tea and have a chat with him at the front gate, and we would always say a respectful "Good Afternoon" if he passed us while we were playing marbles in the gutters on the way home from school.

But Christine didn't want to be like Paper Jack and telling her that Paper Jack would be grateful for her dinner cut no ice at all. She refused point blank to let a green object pass her lips.

In spite of the rowdy meal times we were always cleared away and squashed onto the sofa with a minute to spare before Constable George Dixon said "Good evening, all."

"Aww, it makes me feel all safe to know we 'ave such good men fightin' criminals," Mum Williams sighed. Nobody corrected her. We all knew she hadn't worked out the difference between the news and popular sitcoms when it came to the characters that appeared on her flickering screen. As far as Mum Williams was concerned PC Dixon was on the London beat every single day keeping the people of Britain safe, and PC Andy Crawford was the handsome young man who helped him. Any of the actors playing petty criminals were "rather mean" and if anyone was in a wheelchair or had been hurt in the course of duty, Mum Williams would be genuinely concerned for their well-being and saying things like, "they should tell us which 'ospital 'e's in, then 'ilda could take down a nice cake to get 'im better, poor old sod, they should 'ave let us know!"

Mum Williams became even more confused when there were crime stories in the news that didn't go the way she thought they should. The death sentence passed down to Ruth Ellis was one that she felt law enforcement had got seriously wrong.

"It musta been an accident, a lovely girl like that with two kiddies, there's no way they shoulda 'ung 'er. I wonder why that nice Constable Dixon weren't able to 'elp 'er out …"

We didn't always watch the television, often there was work to be done and everybody had to pitch in.

Although we still had the shop which sold bundles of kindling, bags of potatoes and anthracite nuts – using coal had been frowned on after the deadly smogs of the early 1950s so we had changed over completely to smokeless fuel, which was just as well as anything else became illegal after 1956 – but the shop didn't make much money and there were plenty of mouths to feed. Mum Williams put the word around that we would take in home work and we ended up doing a wide variety of jobs. Sometimes the corridor between the front room and the shop would be full of Harrington's nappies and every evening we would all sit round the table sewing labels into them and listening to the radio. At the end of the evening Nan would package them up in dozens and, once we had finished labelling the entire mountain, a man would come and take them away.

The other job we did frequently was paint lead toys. First we did soldiers in uniforms from the First World War and the Boer War. We intended to create a conveyor belt so that the painting would be done efficiently. Kath opened the first box and unfolded the diagram which showed how each model was meant to be painted, what rank they were and what battalion they were with.

"Right, Margy you sit 'ere, you can paint the 'elmets cos that's the easiest, but nothing else mind. These ones need that dark greeny colour cos they're the safari battalions, and those need grey cos they're in the trenches. 'ilda, sit next to Margy and do them rifles in brown, Mum you do the uniforms and the face colour, then Philip and me'll do the boots and all the details."

Within minutes Hilda was struggling. Her eyes were as bad as her teeth, but her fear of anything medical was so intense that she refused to go and get herself a pair of glasses. She was sure that if she went to any kind of doctor they would tell her she needed to have all her infirmities looked at.

"I can't see this Mum," she said in a whisper.

"Well get out of it then!" Kath growled, "we don't need you messin' everythin' up."

Tears sprang into Hilda's eyes immediately, "Muuum, she's startin' on me again …"

"Stop yer blubbing if you ain't capable of 'elpin', go and find somethin' useful to do … if you can!"

Kath never missed an opportunity to have a dig at Hilda, and Hilda never learnt the art of answering Kath back which would probably have put a stop to it for ever.

"Maybe you could make us all a nice cup o' tea," Mum Williams would say, "it's going to be thirsty work so that would be a very useful thing to do …"

As well as the soldiers we would do farm animals. There were chickens, pigs, cows, sheep, the farmer and the gates to enclose the animals with. Once again the detail work would be done by Kath and Philip and I would be allowed either the pigs or the sheep, whichever one required the least artistic talent.

If we weren't painting or sewing, we would be darning or knitting – or at least everyone apart from me would be knitting.

By now I was a Brownie. I was exceedingly proud of my uniform and knew the Brownie Guide Law by heart. Although Brownies was another expense for Mum Williams, if the other girls in my class were doing it there was no way I was going to miss out on the experience. Mum Williams would get everyone to empty out their pockets on a Friday night and somehow the money would be cobbled together. I was determined to get as many badges sewn onto my sleeve as possible and Brown Owl soon suggested that I try for my Homeworkers badge.

The first part involved darning a sock. Mum Williams was constantly darning Philip's socks and had basketfuls of them that she did for other people. She soon set me up with a wooden mushroom and taught me how to do the basket weave and then go back and forth until the hole was completely filled.

The second task for the badge was to use a knitting doll to make something. These dolls had four pins on their head and a hole down the middle. By weaving wool round the pins and lifting the stitches over them a long tube of knitting came out of the bottom. We used all the scraps of wool that were lying around the house and when the piece was sufficiently long we rolled it round in a circle and Mum Williams sewed it all together to make a teapot stand.

Then came knitting. For some reason I could not get my head, or my hands, around knitting. Although I only had to produce a few squares to make into a doll's blanket, it was the most impossible task I had ever undertaken. I dreaded the part during Brownies when everyone had to take out their handiwork and do some more of it. I was concentrating so hard that my tongue was hanging out of my mouth and each row took an age. As Mum Williams knitted for me between meetings, Tawny Owl would come over and smile, "Margaret O'Callaghan, you're getting on very well with that …" and I would grin up at her while dropping a couple of stitches so Mum Williams would have to sort out another big hole for me when I got home. There was no doubt that many of my Brownie badges were a joint effort!

****

The day for my trip to meet Auntie Peggy and Uncle Noel arrived and I was up hours before the allotted time, dressed in my best clothes with my hair brushed so hard before Mum Williams put it in plaits that it shone in the flickering fire light of the front room.

"You sit by the window then you'll see your Dad's car as soon as it rounds the corner," Mum Williams said as she started peeling the potatoes for Sunday lunch and putting them in a pan of cold salted water. She would walk slowly in and out of the front room doing her morning chores.

"You wait you'll see your Mum and Dad any minute now."

When she went through to the shop to get some more anthracite for the fire I hopped down from the sill to give her a hand.

"You get back up there, you'll get your shoes dirty, they're your best ones and you look pretty as a peach …"

By the time Mum Williams was putting the steam puddings in muslin cloth it was clear my parents were not going to arrive.

"Come on Margy, they're not coming now," Hilda eventually said in her softest voice. "You go and get changed and we'll walk up the road for an ice cream."

As I climbed the stairs to the bedrooms I heard Mum Williams mutter something like "Couple of bloody jokers!" but although it happened several times she never had anything but praise for my parents in front of me.

The motto of the house was, "she's still your muvver, you've only got one muvver, your muvver will always be the most important person to 'er child …" it never wavered, however great the provocation.

****

"Out of bed you lazy lumps!" Cliff was yelling. "The sun's shining! Let's go to the seaside!"

For once it was a properly hot day and we were unlikely be eating sandy sandwiches on a windswept beach whilst trying to convince ourselves this was "bracing". Going to the seaside was a major event. Mum Williams would be last out of the house. Her final act would be to fix her enormous hat on her head with huge hat pins. Even if there was a hurricane, that hat was not going to move. She would stand before the front room mirror and do her hat before shaking all the doors to make sure she had locked them, while we were all waiting at the side of the shop in Kath's big car.

Once we arrived at the coast we would find a sandy spot and then spread out all our stuff. It looked as if we were staying for a week. There was the primus stove, for a nice cup of tea, great stripy windbreakers that had to be anchored all around us, tins of sandwiches, plus a tin of cold potatoes, pies and rock cakes, we certainly weren't going to go hungry.

While Mum Williams would remain wrapped in her gabardine coat and expansive hat, the children would be helped to wriggle into saggy knitted swimming costumes beneath one of the outsized Welling Municipal bath towels. We ensured that nobody could see an inch of our flesh while we changed, and Hilda would look away while she held our towels when we eventually struggled out of our wet costumes and back into our knickers.

We weren't allowed to go far from our base camp, but unfortunately Christine slipped on some stones and made a hole in her bathing costume, so she spent the rest of the day sitting down so that nobody would see her bottom. The rest of the children continued to run backwards and forwards from the sea with buckets to feed the moat around the sandcastle we had made, as the sun beat down on our fair, bare heads.

The burns we suffered were so bad we couldn't go to school for three days. I remember I couldn't wear normal clothes because by the time I woke up the following day the blisters were so large I could tip my arm one way and another to watch the liquid slosh about inside them. I lived in one of the vests Aunty Vi had brought over from the Turkish Baths. It was silky and a peach colour. On my child's body it was like a nightdress. Hilda was given some foul smelling powder by the doctor that Mum Williams dusted us with every hour. We were in such a state that there was no way she could dab the blisters with calamine.

Eventually the burns became less angry and I was able to return to school. Still, nobody knew how to prevent sunburn, so it was lucky we lived in a climate where it almost never became hot enough to happen.

****

Mum Williams was pragmatic about illness, especially things like chickenpox. If one child got the virus she would put all of us in the same room together so we all got it over and done with. When I became covered in itchy spots, Christine, Tina, Trevor and Jaqueline soon followed suit. We knew we were really ill because Mum Williams sent Hilda up the road for some Lucozade which was 2'6d a bottle. Mum Williams was now in her late sixties, she hobbled constantly, we had no running hot water, no washing machine, everything had to be done by hand, yet she would care for a bunch of feverish children, regularly dabbing them all with calamine lotion, while the babies needed nursing through the night as well. Admittedly if Mum Williams was up throughout the small hours, so was Hilda, but she at least had youth on her side.

In general our health was good compared to previous generations. We all had a third of a pint of milk given to us at school each day – frozen in the winter and curdled in the summer, but the rest of the time it was drinkable. When my sisters were young we were also given free orange juice at the antenatal clinic which was held in the church hall at St Andrews. By the time Christine started school we had the polio vaccine too and seeing children in leg irons was becoming rare.

****

Ivy and Cliff had only been married about a year when the whole household was woken up to find ambulance men thundering up the stairs. Cliff was in a blind panic and even Kath was in a state of disarray. Ivy had suffered a massive asthma attack. It was the first one she had ever experienced, but unfortunately it was not her last and from that night onwards she was almost an invalid from the disease.

Having children was out of the question now, which was a harsh blow for the newly weds. When they moved into their own home on the other side of Duppas Hill, Cliff had to undertake all the cleaning, gardening and heavy work. Their home was on the ground floor because Ivy could not have managed stairs; also it was close to Ivy's office so she could still get to work. They made one of the rooms into my bedroom and I would often walk back to their house with them after Friday family dinner at 21A and spend the weekend there until we all went to West Street for Sunday lunch.

So now I had two homes where I had a bed and a warm welcome, even if I had not yet seen where my own parents lived.

****

Around this time I acquired my third home. My best friend at school was Mary Nightingale. She came from a completely conventional family which I found endlessly fascinating. Mary and her brother Graham both had proper beds in separate bedrooms. Their parents ran a normal home where you would be asked: "Would you like to sit up now …" for tea, and people didn't shout most of the time. It was a bit of a revelation and seemed immensely genteel and grown up.

Mrs Nightingale always used to support me, as well as Mary, in school plays or other local activities. Increasingly frequently Mum Williams found it too hard on her legs to come up to the school on parents' days, although she was endlessly proud of all of the children's achievements and displayed any cups or ribbons we won in her best room upstairs. However, if I needed active support on sports day Mrs Nightingale had the loudest voice south of London and could be guaranteed to be an enthusiastic audience at every race. In fact, if I needed anything Mrs Nightingale's door was always open. They knew I had an unusual home life, but although I was unlikely to be able to invite Mary to my house more than once a year, for my birthday tea, they invited me to their home almost every week.

The father of one of my other friends, Wendy, had a motorbike with a sidecar, so I coveted invitations to her home for a completely different reason. Wheels! Although I loved her house, especially as she had plenty of modern toys plus a room of her own where we could play quietly with them, it was the ride home in her Dad's sidecar that was the highlight of any visit.

The sidecar was shaped like a bullet with a brown leather interior and a little half circle windscreen. Although most people just jumped in, I liked opening the mini door and stepping in while arranging my hat and gloves which Mum Williams insisted I wore if I were going on the bike. Usually Wendy would ride behind her father on the bike itself, but occasionally we would change places and I loved that too. It was wonderful that "health and safety" hadn't been invented by then. My experiences riding on Kath's luggage rack on the back of her giant car, on the motorbike and in the sidecar, plus racing the many go-carts that carpenter Charlie made for Philip and me out of orange boxes, string and old pram wheels, were shining points of pure pleasure in my speed-happy life.

****

Charlie and Cliff were trying to drag Mum Williams into the twentieth century by installing a gas cooker in her kitchen. They both gave her careful demonstrations of how to use it and assured her it was far easier to turn one small knob and use one match rather than fire up the big old range with kindling and coke.

"When it's summer you don't want that big old range heating the place up," Charlie reasoned, "it will save you half an hour in the mornings not 'aving to get that thing fired up."

Mum Williams looked dubious but agreed to give it a go to keep the boys happy.

“’ilda, get across to the butchers for a couple of shoulders of lamb so’s I can stuff ‘em for dinner.”

Looking warily at the new world contraption that was now in her kitchen, she sat at the table pounding herbs and vegetables together ready to stuff and roll the meat so that it would stretch as far as possible.

“’ere you are Mum,” Hilda said as she breezed back in before heading off to work.

“’ow much did she charge you for that?”

“That was one and three Mum …”

“Daylight robbery! Oh ‘ilda, look at that! There’s no meat on that!”

I don’t think I ever heard anybody say, “that’s great, thanks” to Hilda. She always seemed to be in the wrong whatever she did.

Although Mum Williams tried to keep the men out of the kitchen, the lamb rolls and everything else still kept coming out of the range. Cliff and Charlie soon found out and eventually they put a huge piece of wood in front of the range to train Mum Williams into using the gas stove. It was only balanced in place, so she still persuaded someone take it down when the weather became cold and she needed to heat the house, but for the most part she was forced to change her ways.

The two husbands were part of the family, and they were men, so they were allowed to cajole the matriarch into a few alterations despite her advancing years. However there was about to be a third man join the household. By virtue of his gender alone, none of the women would openly oppose Cyril, but nevertheless they loathed him unanimously. The only way they felt able to demonstrate this was to forbid him from ever using the front door or the front room.

Chapter Six

Hilda was in her mid-thirties when she met Cyril Wakeman. By trade he was an electrician, a sparky, but in reality he did a number of jobs including working in a furniture shop. The two of them probably met at work; certainly she never went out with him in the conventional way, for a start Mum Williams wouldn't have allowed her to be away from the house when she had chores to be done.

Cyril wasn't blessed with good looks. He had stained angry teeth. His incisors were longer than the rest which gave him the appearance of a cinematic vampire and he spoke with his jaw clenched. He was tall with a mass of dark brown hair and black bushy eyebrows that curled upwards in random places. His bottom jaw was bigger than the top one which probably exacerbated his speech problems. He appeared dirty and, although he was not particularly heavy, he suffered from weeping leg ulcers throughout his life. I have no idea what colour his eyes were as I never dared to look into them.

Hilda's man was incapable of stringing a sentence together without swear words. If you took three words that he had said and wrote them down verbatim there would only be one normal word to pick out, the rest was cussing. Mum Williams used to swear, but she didn't think it was swearing and that seemed to make all the difference. She'd say "Oh bugger it" a lot and "Gaw blimey" but she never used "fuck" and "shit" which were constant currency out of Cyril's mouth. Kath and Hilda never swore at all, so this was shocking stuff. He also couldn't say the name "Martina" so it was always, "'Art, oi, err you …"

His sole redeeming feature was that he had a motorbike and an Austin 7. It was through these useful items that Cyril managed to begin moving in on the family. He would be sent off to do errands if Kath and her car weren't available. He was also roped into taking me to the Children's Cinema Club every Saturday morning.

Most of the kids my age would go to the CCC. It was more than just watching films, we frequently had a magician, and would be encouraged to get up and do some singing, plus there would be quizzes with sweets as rewards for those who got the answers correct. The club allowed a large number of parents to have some peace on a Saturday morning because it was inexpensive and the children actually wanted to attend.

Once Cyril had begun ingratiating himself by helping out, his next move was to try and impress us any way he could.

The furniture store where he worked also did removals and deliveries. Many years after he first arrived at 21A, Cyril and a couple of other men were sent over to Charlie Watt's house to deliver some chairs. Admittance into the house of one of The Rolling Stones morphed into Cyril's fifteen minutes of fame. Every one of us was told, on innumerable occasions, "Yer, I know dem Stones ..." a phrase that was usually accompanied by a nonchalant slouch. This may have impressed Hilda, but Mum Williams had no idea who The Rolling Stones were, and whatever Cyril did was anathema to Kath who was irritated beyond words at having her home invaded by someone so loutish.

Even with the ban on Cyril to the main areas of the house, he wasn't about to be put off by the cold shoulder. He retained his lodgings in a building several streets away but would be there as little as possible. At the beginning of their relationship Hilda would entertain him in the unenticing environment of the shop, which was almost closed by this stage. If Cyril harboured expectations that he would eventually be invited into the front room to eat with the rest of the family, he was endlessly disappointed.

Every Friday it appeared as if Mum Williams was cooking for the whole of Croydon – apart from Cyril. There were lots of extra children around, not just Trevor and Jacqueline, but others whose parents would "just drop them off for an hour or two while I get a few things done for the weekend", or young mothers who would "just park the pram here while I run to the shops". By the time I arrived home from school, Philip would be trying to read quietly among the mayhem of babies and toddlers. Mum Williams would already have produced piles of cakes and scones and would be on to the savouries. If Philip and I sloped off to race our go-carts we would always return by the time the factory workers arrived home. Ivy and Hilda would bang through the front gate a little before Kath, Marjory, Charlie and Cliff. Slowly the various extra children would be spirited away with a "Thanks Mrs Williams!", and Nell would put the final delicacy of the day onto the stove.

Slowly she would bring her pigs trotters to the boil and an interesting aroma would pervade the house as she simmered them until the flesh began to fall off the bones. Mum Williams had long since lost all the teeth in her head, but she loved to suck the flesh from boiled pigs trotters, it was her Friday night treat. While the rest of us tucked into the mountain of food she had made, she would settle herself on the sofa with the bowl of trotters in front of her, and begin slurping. It was the only mealtime when she did not sit at the table with everyone else, but then Friday evenings were special.

When the trotters were exhausted we arrived at the time when I would be sent to the off-license. Kath would come to the kitchen door and give me half a crown and send me to buy her a bottle of VP port and an arrowroot biscuit. They cost tuppence and were the size of a side plate, slightly savoury and thick.

"I'm goin' over the road for Kath's port, does anyone else want anythin'?" I would ask the crowd in the front room, sometimes they would want a bottle of beer and some lemonade to make shandies, but they weren't big drinkers.

Mum Williams would lay out the Croydon Advertiser and begin to work her way through the births, deaths and marriages, and the cosy evening would be regularly punctuated with, "Do you remember so and so … 'e's gone."

Kath would continue bashing around in the kitchen until the first half of her bottle of port was consumed. Then she would move into the front room with her arrowroot biscuit and the rest of the port bottle. Sitting in the corner on a high backed chair in her trousers and turban, she would roll a cigarette and blow the smoke into the kitchen. Apart from my father, she was the only one of the family who smoked.

Once the final piece of gossip had been extracted and dissected from the Croydon Advertiser, Nell would begin to rock gently. It was a sign they all recognised.

"What's the matter Mum? What do you want?"

There would be a pause and then she would say something like, "Christine needs new shoes…" or "Margy has a school trip to pay for…"

"Right, come on then," one of them would say and they would get out an envelope and write "Christine's Shoes" or "Margy's Trip" on it before passing it round and putting in whatever they could – even Marjory and Charlie, who had two children of their own to support, chipped in. My parents never visited on a Friday evening, for predictable reasons.

Once Cyril got the message that he was never going to be welcomed into the front room, he employed a new tactic.

Kath regularly painted the kitchen walls with green distemper. It was an early form of whitewash made from powdered chalk or lime with a binding agent of gelatine. It was meant to give a textured finish, but under Kath's hand it was merely lumpy.

We no longer had the rabbits as most of them had been wiped out by Myxomatosis, and we had also stopped keeping turkeys so we didn't use the cellar to house livestock in the winter months. The shop was no longer a thriving business and less fuel was stored in the cellar due to the fantastic modern gas cooker taking over from the range, so Cyril hit on the idea of cleaning up the cellar and painting it with distemper. It was a plan that was hard not to like, especially for Kath, whose weekly bath would be considerably enhanced by the new décor.

Cyril scrubbed and painted, then finished off by moving an old sofa down there together with a lamp, a small oil fire and a radio. The couple had their love nest.

Every evening after tea had been cleared away, Hilda would descend into the basement while the rest of us snuggled under Mum William's brown blanket, killed the lights and watched the tiny flickering TV screen. When the first sci-fi programmes were shown the monsters scared the hell out of us and we would spend most of the programme with the blanket pulled over our heads.

"It's all gone now," Kath would say, just in time to ensure we opened our eyes at the worst possible moment.

Our viewing would usually be punctuated, at least twice, by Hilda emerging from the cellar steps, looking like a blind pit pony, empty teapot in hand as she tripped her way across everybody's outstretched legs to get to the kitchen.

"Oh Margy .. Oh sorry Mum …" she'd cry as the huge shadow of the teapot jerked across the TV screen – the sole shaft of light in our blacked-out room.

"Careful everyone," Kath would interject, "Bear's breath is out of 'er lair!"

Hilda would start crying again and Mum Williams would try to calm things down with "Now then Kath …" as Hilda vanished into the kitchen and made a fresh pot of tea.

The same scenario would be enacted on her way back down to the cellar, by which time Kath would have thought up a new insult, usually relating to how much Hilda had let herself go since she started seeing Cyril.

When the programmes lost their appeal and Christine and Tina had quietly fallen asleep on the sofa, Mum Williams would hobble over to the top of the cellar steps and yell, "'ilda! 'ilda! What you doin' down there! 'ilda, these two little-uns want t'go t'bed," and Hilda would be dragged back to her daily reality of looking after Flora's children before falling asleep in her brown armchair beneath a pile of coats. Cyril would exit. He was never allowed to stay in the house past ten thirty at night.

If Mum Williams was ever feeling a little drowsy, Kath would ensure the routine was stuck to.

"Mum! 'ave you seen the time Mum? 'e's still down there you know! I don't know what they're doin' down there! Can you imagine! I'd love to be a fly on the wall …" all of which was guaranteed to get Mum Williams into an impressive fluster as she made an arthritic sprint for the cellar steps.

"'ilda! What time do you call this! It's time you were up here now! I don't know what you're doin' down there!"

The notion that her daughters were adults at twenty-one, or even thirty-one, was not something Mum Williams subscribed to.

****

Our house was next to the church, and the church was a huge part of our lives. All the rituals and festivals that kept communities together were rigorously observed. I would always go to church on Sunday afternoon and when I was older we used to go to Sunday School as well, this was held in the first few pews of the Lady Chapel. All of us would have our poppies pinned to our lapels for Remembrance Day as soon as the first one hit the high street, and wherever we were in the house, as the clock struck eleven on the eleventh of November we would stand stock still, in silence, for two long minutes. We did the full gamut of advent before Christmas plus Shrove Tuesday and Ash Wednesday before Lent.

At Harvest Festival we would get crêpe paper and orange boxes from Freddy Moseley, the greengrocer over the road. The green paper would be put all the way around the handles to make a big bow and then we would collect things like oranges, apples and bananas plus tins of peaches and tomatoes until the boxes looked extravagantly full.

The boxes were given to the poor families of the parish of which, if the truth were known, we were one. If our offerings weren't fit for a king, Nell wouldn't let them go out of the house.

"I'm not 'aving people talk about us. That looks paltry that does. 'ere, shove anover banana in."

We would be sent off to the festival, three little girls, beautifully dressed, each with a sumptuous box. When we arrived back home Nell would say, "Nuffin' for me! No, they don't give nuffin' to me do they! You want to tell 'em I'm 'ere you know!"

What we *did* know was that she would have died of shame if anyone had ever given her a box. We might be poor, but we made up for it with lashings of pride.

The biggest church event for us children was May Day. Every year we had different colours for our satin May Day dresses and breeches. Each of the local churches named a King and Queen with all the other children being their maids and pages. If St Andrew's was using purple one year, then St. Mary's might use blue and the children from All Saints could be in red or green. The headdresses we used were usually taken apart each year and then put back in a different form by the families as Spring began, the family might also make our sashes, but the main dress-making was done by special ladies from the church and we would have to go for at least two fittings, and be pricked by innumerable pins, before the big day.

The night before the May Day weekend the three of us would go to bed with our hair tightly wound round rags to give us pretty ringlets beneath our flower-laden coronets. Mum Williams would have instigated a new whip-round-envelope marked "May Queen" to pay for our lace gloves, white buckskin sandals and little white socks. On the Saturday morning we would all gather at the big church of St Peter before being split roughly into age groups and going off to perform our various duties. I would be with Mary Nightingale and our other friends. Often we visited retirement homes and took gifts to the old people, or sang a few songs to an array of nodding white heads.

One year we took gifts round to the Shirley Oaks children's home. This made quite an impact on me. All the children who lived there didn't have families to care for them or buy them white buckskin sandals.

They lived in a succession of separate "houses" with a house mother and a house father for every ten or twelve kids. The whole place seemed very cold, all the drainpipes and doors were painted a uniform green colour and the children were very formal and called their carers "House Mother" or "House Father". It was clear that discipline was strict as they didn't seem like real children, they were too reserved. A very solemn girl of about fourteen showed us around her house which seemed to be unnaturally tidy for a place that contained a dozen children. I found it shocking that the Shirley Oaks kids were all wearing their school uniforms despite the fact that it was a Saturday afternoon. I never saw hide nor hair of my uniform over the weekend because as soon as I went through the front door on Friday afternoon it was whipped off me in order to be washed and ironed ready for Monday morning. The whole orphanage experience made me rather pensive, but not because I identified with the children in any way.

After our duties, there would be dancing in the church hall around the May Pole, parades and church services. Eventually we would go back to the hall to find it filled with trestle tables all laid out with our May Day tea. Prizes would be awarded for the best-dressed Queen before our finery was returned to the church to see which bits could be unpicked and reused the following year.

****

Although I would be dressed up in my finery with all the rest of the children for these events, I still had one eye in the pot and the other up the chimney, so a further eye operation was scheduled. Mum Williams hated to see us in any discomfort and she would be wringing her hands for days beforehand, telling all the passing neighbours at the fence that the "Poor little gal 'as got to 'ave anover one."

All the operations, after the first one, took place at the May Day clinic. Kath would drive us up there and Hilda would be detailed to accompany me into the pale green land of disinfectant, despite the fact that she was mortally terrified of anything to do with medicine. However, Mum Williams was similarly scared and was firmly glued to her car seat, so Hilda had no choice.

I might be allowed a day off school after a visit to the hospital but more pampering than that was unlikely. There was the School Board Man to consider.

The threat of the School Board Man was like the threat of "I'll fetch a policeman", nothing ever happened, but the threat was useful. Our School Board Man used to ride around with his battered brief case strapped to the crossbar of his bike. He always wore glasses and bicycle clips, plus a hat and an off-brown overcoat in winter. He knew our family and would always say "Morning Mrs Williams" as he cycled passed the gate, at which point if any of us were late, or whining for a day off, one of the aunts would say, "'e's seen you now, you've got to get to school extra quick!"

I reckon he had more work in Old Town than around our streets. That was the area where the tenement blocks stood, each with one tap per landing. The tenements were condemned for demolition at the end of the war, but they were still standing with families swarming through them throughout most of the 1950s. Old Town was recognised as being a bad area. Southbridge Street used to run through Old Town but it also extended passed our home, even though we were classed as West Street. Mum Williams was very sensitive to this fact and if anybody had the temerity to say "Oh, you live in Old Town …" she would draw herself up to her full diminutive height, stare them straight in the eye and growl, "We do NOT live in Old Town, we live in South Croydon!" before turning on her heel and hobbling away from the offensive person with as much grace as she could muster.

****

When I was about nine the day finally arrived when I was taken to meet my Uncle Noel and Auntie Peggy. That Sunday my father's car really did come around the corner and stop as I sat dressed and ready on the window sill. I was bundled into the back seat in a haze of excitement and spent the journey down to the coast half expecting to be taken somewhere else.

Auntie Peggy had a more pronounced Irish accent than my father. She never had any children but had married into a family that was far wealthier than her own had been. Noel Etches was part Italian. Handsome and charming, he was once Mayor of Peacehaven.

Despite being childless they lived in a six bedroomed house with turrets, leaded windows and great glass doors that led into a garden that was terraced up a hill and topped with a beautiful wooden summer house. Behind the summer house was their own private wood where they walked their dogs.

Uncle Noel was a big, fun-loving man who knew how to handle my mother like nobody else. Flora could sulk for Britain if anyone even said "hello" in a tone she didn't like. My father spent his entire married life trying to make her laugh, to stop her from sulking. She needed to be constantly flattered or bad atmospheres were guaranteed.

When our car arrived, Uncle Noel flew out of the front gate and swept open the passenger side door.

"My goodness Flora, you look well, I love that hat on you …" he said taking her hand as if she were royalty and helping her step from the car. From that moment on he could do no wrong.

My aunt sauntered out and I fell instantly in love with both of them.

"Hey Kiddo!" she said, as if we had known each other for years and I was as cool as she obviously was.

Auntie Peggy was pretty in an elfin way with a round face, short browny-red hair that had a natural curl and painted fingernails. She wore bright lipstick and slightly shiny white trousers that had stirrups under the feet to pull them down. She was slim and, by British standards, her face and arms were exotically tanned. Her smile oozed with calm; it was as if nothing could ruffle her. This last quality probably annoyed my mother more than anything else.

My first day with my Uncle and Aunt was paradise. They listened to me like an adult whilst indulging me like a child. Noel was careful not to overstep the mark and make my mother jealous through lack of attention. She flirted with him constantly but would not allow my father to drift off with his sister. I, however, was less important and was not stopped from creeping into the kitchen to help my aunt with the washing up after a lunch that was unlike anything I had ever seen at 21A West Street.

Not that we were badly fed by Mum Williams, far from it, but there was no finesse. Usually both of her slightly grubby thumbs would be wallowing in the gravy as she carried the laden plates through to the front room and banged them down before us. If we didn't eat everything up that was on our plates, it would just be served up to us again for the next meal.

Peggy and Noel's home was a world away from all that. However, Peggy, like Mum Williams, had been in service before she married. Through this she had learnt all the things required to run a posh house, although at that time she never expected to have one of her own. She taught me about not putting bone-handled cutlery in water, how to fold napkins to look like shells and a host of other dainty details that she employed to make her own home seem effortlessly elegant.

When the time came to leave, my aunt and uncle ruffled my hair in a genuinely affectionate manner.

"Try to have grown longer nails by the time you come again!" Peggy said as I climbed into the car. It was the encouragement I needed to make a proper effort to stop biting them. They were effectively saying to my parents that they should bring me again. I was in heaven.

****

I never stopped recounting everything that had happened to me on my day with Peggy and Noel, and while the adults at 21A all humoured me, it was clearly getting up Christine's nose.

Christine was about three years old and did not like the idea of being left out, or being lumped in with Tina while I went gallivanting around the country with our parents – once!

"Auntie Peggy will like me more than you cos we have the same colour hair!" she said. Tina and I both had white blonde hair like my mother, but Christine looked like our father. Her conviction that she would shine to Noel and Peggy in comparison to me wasn't particularly annoying, but when she started taunting that she would tell our mother of my various misdemeanours, "and then they won't take you with them again", I began to see red.

The next time Flora was enjoying her first cup of tea with Kath, Christine whispered the fateful words, "I'm gonna tell Mum on you ..." I'd had enough.

Grabbing a pair of scissors from Mum Williams' needlework box, I held Christine's small arm tightly and marched her out of the back door before she had a chance to open her mouth. By the time she realised she should yell, ninety per cent of her hair was on the ground behind Kath's car.

Kath, Mum Williams and finally my own mother, came out of the house to see what the commotion was about. Flora pulled her mouth tightly together and hit me hard across the back of the legs.

"You're a naughty girl, a naughty, naughty girl! Just look at what you've done!"

While ignoring any need to comfort Christine, she went completely berserk with me. It was as if I had scarred my sister for life. My hacking made Christine look a bit of an urchin, and with Flora everything was about show. She might not pay for her children, but she liked the fact that they were always turned out nicely. It reflected well on her. She left the house swiftly in a state of righteous indignation, vowing not to visit again until I had learnt how to behave, which sent Christine into a fresh bout of hysteria.

I was embarrassed and unhappy, but when Hilda came home things got worse.

"Oh Mum, look what she's done to 'er 'air! What a little bitch! Just look what she's done!"

This was said in a state of breathless admiration, whilst inside I was begging Hilda to stop going on.

In fact, Mum Williams thought Flora's reaction to the situation was hilarious. "It'll grow back," she said, "I don't know what she's carpin' on about s' much!"

They sat Christine up on the kitchen table and began to tidy up my art work while Kath propped up the doorframe smoking a roll-up.

"Well, she's definitely not goin' to be a Mr. Teezy Weezy," she said, referring to one of the first television hairdressers who had a huge moustache, was cringingly smarmy, and used to do the hair for international beauty pageants, "and it's not as if any of us see Flora regular, so it will probably 'ave grown back by the time she pitches up again."

As it turned out, we were destined to see far more of my parents from then on.

Chapter Seven

I arrived home from school to find my father in animated conversation with Mum Williams.

"I cannot understand for the life of me why some people have to be so h-interfering," my father was saying, as Mum Williams moved towards the kitchen before emerging with a rock cake and a large blob of jam on a plate.

"'ere y' are Margy, I done it all nice wiv the jam."

"What's happening, Mum?" I asked.

"You and yer sisters will be spending weekends with yer Mum and Dad from now on," she said smiling down at me. "Won't that be nice."

I thought about it. I was intrigued to see where they lived but I wasn't sure I fancied a permanent arrangement. I would hate to have missed the previous weekend. I had spent much of it with Philip and Uncle Cliff up at the air show. Croydon airport was proud of its Amy Johnson heritage and used to offer spectacular days out for local people. As both Philip and Cliff were mad on planes I used to be taken to the Open Air Days regularly. I also wouldn't want to miss the picnics we all went on. I loved helping Mum Williams line the big biscuit tins with muslin or clean tea towels and then stuffing them full of pork pies, potatoes and hard boiled eggs before we headed out blackberry-ing or to the beach. I would also spend whole weekends at Cliff and Ivy's house where they had given me my own pretty room which led out onto their garden. Then I had a shocking thought ...

"But it's my birthday in a fortnight, I don't have to be away from home then do I?"

My father looked bewildered, "Is it? Do you want to stay here for that?"

"Aw, she's worried about 'er burfday tea," Mum Williams explained. "I'm sure yer Mum will do you a lover-ly burfday tea Margy."

"With a green jelly rabbit on brown blancmange? And candles? And can Mary Nightingale and Wendy Gater come round?"

"Well, it might not be egg-sackly the same, Margy, but I'm sure you'll like it just as much."

"I don't believe it would be a problem if they missed birthday weekends, we've only got to show the council that we have children, we don't need them every single weekend" my father interjected. I breathed a huge sigh of relief. I wouldn't miss the balloons and party games or the iced Victoria sponge cake after all.

Christine and Tina wandered into the front room with cotton wool protruding from their ears. They seemed to have constant ear infections and I wondered if our mother would remember to do their ears on the nights we stayed at her house.

Once I had secured my birthday tea I lost interest in the conversation. My father left swiftly once he had arranged to pick us up at six o'clock on Friday evening. Then Mum Williams explained the situation in minute detail to each one of her daughters when they arrived home, so, although I was trying to listen to Children's Hour with Uncle Mac on the radio, I got the gist of why we were being sent.

"It's a bit of a worry for 'em, one of their neighbours went and told on them to the council. Looks like they was jealous of the big 'ouse they 'ave. Asked the council why Gerard 'ad a free bedroomed corner 'ouse when they don't 'ave no kids. 'e went up the council and says the children are at boardin' school an' that's why the neighbours never see nothin', but the council lady says 'they're only there in the 'olidays then?', an' she's thinking they don't need that big 'ouse if the kids are 'ardly ever there, so 'e 'as to turn on the charm and says they comes 'ome every weekend, but they are so well be'aved the neighbour never noticed them! 'e's goin' to pick 'em up after work every Friday and Kath's goin' to pick 'em up again on a Sunday afternoon. It'll be a bit of a change, but maybe I can get their eiderdowns washed and give 'em a bit of a re-stitch if they're away for a night or two now an' again."

Directly Uncle Mac was over we were scooted out of the front room so that Mum Williams could squeeze Kath's boils.

Kath had a regular problem with boils. They were usually on her back or her bottom and Mum Williams would make up bread poultices to dress them. Everyone in our household was exceedingly modest. The family went to sleep in their clothes, and when they changed into something fresh it would be done in complete privacy, so exposing Kath's back ensured that the curtains were drawn and nobody was allowed in the room from either the kitchen or the hall until everything was over.

There was no anaesthetic available, so we would hear Kath's screams wherever we were on the property. Once they had been lanced open Mum Williams would have to squeeze and squeeze until everything was out, including the core. At the end of the sounds of torment, we might hear Kath's exhausted voice saying, "Did you get it Mum? Did you get the core?" When the core was out it was unlikely the boil would return and Kath could feel that all the pain she had been through was worth it. If Mum Williams hadn't managed to get the core, Kath would have a hunted look on her face throughout the evening, while the rest of them would be discussing the gory details.

"Ooo, it were ever so green this time Kath, and thick, like cold custard..."

Although we didn't see it, not a lot was left to the imagination.

While we had been outside listening to Kath's agony, Hilda had announced she had a treat for me now that I wouldn't be around as much at the weekends.

"We'll go an' see *The King an' I*, an' pay full price for the posh seats, an' have an ice cream an' all," she said. I was delighted. Maybe going to my parents' house would be fun and I would get extra treats for being away. The prospects were improving by the minute. I had been looking at the posters for *The King and I* for weeks and hoping Hilda might suggest going, I already knew some of the songs and I couldn't wait to see the extravagant costumes on the big screen.

It was a busy week what with school, the cinema and also an invitation to come round to play from Cynthia Shakespeare. Although Cynthia was closer to Christine's age than mine we got on well and I don't think the girls from her private school were keen on visiting her home because Shakespeares were the local undertakers. When I was small and out running errands with Kath, she would often hold me up to the frosted glass of Shakespeare's window and growl in my ear, "There's dead bodies in there ..." so initially I was apprehensive about visiting the place. However, by the grand old age of nine I knew there was nothing ghastly on show and the only down side was a lingering perfume of formaldehyde. When I arrived back home Mum Williams would take one sniff, throw open all the windows and say, "I can tell you've been down Shakespeare's again!"

Before I knew it, Friday school was over, my uniform was being pummelled against the washboard while I was standing on the curb with a cloth bag hanging off one shoulder, containing a change of under clothes for each of us plus our toothbrushes and a flannel. With the small hand of a sister in each of my larger ones, we waited for my father's car to arrive.

Driving through the countryside that lapped up against Croydon, we were soon purring down Hedley Drive. Half way along the street my father pulled over in front of a big council house with a wild garden that wrapped itself right round the house.

"Cor Dad! How many bedrooms does it have?" I said in wonder.

"There's three, so your sisters can share the big one and you can have the box room all to yourself," he said as he got out of the car and released us from the fug of his cigarette smoke into the clean country air. "Better than Nell's hovel, eh?"

I didn't answer. Not even with a nod. I loved my home. It wasn't that I was comparing my parents' house with Mum Williams', they were two separate things in my mind and I didn't like them being crushed together.

Inside the house was neat and exceedingly clean. The kitchen was modern with compact built-in units and shiny surfaces. It was different in every way from what I was accustomed to, we seemed to have stepped into another world. The lounge was smaller than our front room and not nearly as brown but there was a separate dining room as well as the lounge, just for eating in. The lounge itself seemed cramped. The sofa and two armchairs were touching one another as they were pushed as close to the fireplace as possible in a semi-circle.

The upstairs was framed by a landing with a broad solid bannister around it. In the corner there was the toilet, and next to it a splendid indoor bathroom. The back double bedroom came next, and then my parents' bedroom with the box room at the end. There were two single beds in my parents' room which my mother had ordered before they moved in, after Tina was born when the doctors had found the shadow on her lung. Flora was convinced she would not survive another pregnancy so, as my father was a Catholic, there was only one solution.

I didn't understand any of this at the time of course, having been raised in a household run by someone brought up in the full blast of Victorian prudishness. I just saw the two single beds, neatly made with clean candlewick bedspreads.

I placed the change of clothes for Christine and Tina in the back bedroom and took the rest of the bag into the box room where I would be sleeping for the next two nights. When my mother arrived home from the Sleepeasy factory the house began to fill with the delicious aroma of breaded fish. It was so wonderful that it even overpowered the constant smell of my father's cigarettes.

"You look beautiful Flora," my Dad was saying as I entered the kitchen, "is that a new dress?"

"With all this extra work to keep our 'ouse, I tret myself," she replied, deftly scooping the fish onto five separate plates. "Margaret, please lay the table, the potatoes are nearly ready. Tomorrow morning you can stay with the children," she said turning to my Dad. "I need to 'ave my hair done and relax a bit after all the strain I've been under."

I discovered that my mother was a rather good cook. Nothing fancy, but she used new expensive things that we had never tasted before like Cornflakes and fish fingers. Our first meal at my parents' house wasn't awkward. Dad was in full Irish flow with his jokes and his many stories, he was lapping up his new eager audience. He told us he was a partner in a garage, "as well as having a finger in a good many other pies as well!"

We were impressed.

By the time he got on to his war stories all three of us were sitting in open-mouthed wonder.

"My battalion was in the middle of France, there were no signposts so that the enemy was as much in the dark as we were, and the maps weren't worth the paper used to print them! Indeed they weren't! We got to a crossroads and my commanding officer was turning the map round and about trying to get an idea of where we were.

"It's left, Sir" I says to him.

"Have you been here before O'Callaghan?" he asks me.

"No, but I just know it's that way," I says.

"He chewed on his pipe for a full minute before saying, "I hope the stories about canny Irishmen are right," and waved at me to turn left. I could feel it in my sinews it was the right course. I reckon it was my dear dead brother keeping us safe, because it turned out if we had gone right we would have run straight into an enemy ambush. Ah yes, there's many things we don't understand in this world and others who have gone before us guide us through …"

Almost as soon as tea was over our Mother started to yawn. I did the drying up while she washed and then we watched Double Your Money in the lounge. Just before it ended Mum announced she was too tired to watch anymore and was going to bed. She went upstairs but a few minutes later returned with her nightdress in her hand.

Standing with her back to the fire, her unknown children and husband ranged in front of her, she removed every stitch of clothing, carefully folded each piece and then, finally, put on her nightdress. She was so close to us I could have put out my hand and touched her stomach. I wanted to look away but I was shocked and fascinated all at the same time. Her striptease revealed a tiny bust above an enormous wrinkly stomach. The wrinkles spanned the entire abdomen and were held up by two sturdy legs which were bridged by a small triangle of blonde hair.

"Don't wake me when you come in Gerard," she said as she eased herself out between our chairs. "See you all in the morning."

There was far more room in my parents' house than at 21A, yet somehow we saw far more of the adults than we had ever done in the past. We quickly discovered that my father never closed the loo door, whatever he was doing. When we walked up the stairs we were regularly confronted by his back view and the loud sound of liquid hitting water from a height, or his seated face, trousers around his ankles, and even more graphic accompaniments. The two of them were used to living in their house by themselves, where none of the modesty we had been brought up with was needed.

Although my mother went to bed ridiculously early in the evenings, she made up for it by rising at five in the morning and beginning to bang around the house to ensure that most of us were completely awake by six.

"Your mother always walks abroad in the small hours," our father confided with a grin, "it's another cross we have to bear!"

By Saturday night I was missing my home. The house felt strange and unwelcoming. I wanted the familiarity of the brown blanket on Mum Williams' sofa, the smell of Kath's room and my bed's cosy heaviness from the old overcoats that kept me warm. Everything was unfamiliar and I still had another twenty-four hours before I could get back to normality. I went to bed unhappy, expecting to wake up to a boring, but weird, Sunday.

Sundays at Mum Williams' house were a round of church, Sunday lunch and a quiet afternoon. There were strict rules governing play on the Lord's Day. No playing outside, no noisy games, no hanging washing outside or doing any unnecessary household chores at all, no friends calling. It was a family day, a day for quiet reflection, as much as was possible in our crowded home.

"You've got acres of room to play outside in the garden," my father announced once the breakfast dishes had been washed. "I don't want you in the house getting under your mother's feet and bothering her."

We didn't need telling twice, it felt deliciously immoral to enjoy a noisy game of hide-and-seek on a Sunday.

A girl with auburn hair of about my age came out of the next door house and began to watch us. Eventually she moved closer to the fence and held up her hand in a wave, we went over to her.

"Hello, I'm Patsy, have you just moved in?"

We gave her the lie about living elsewhere during the week because of school and invited her to join our game. When it began to rain heavily we stood around wondering what to do. Mum was busy cooking Sunday lunch so we wouldn't be welcome in the house.

"You can all come round to my house, my Mum won't mind." So we trotted off to meet our new neighbours.

Rita Hopper, Patsy's mum, was about the same age as our mother, but she looked completely different. Slim and very good looking, she was made up to the nines, dressed in a tight short skirt with seamed stockings leading upwards from her six inch heels with winkle-picker toes. Rita's husband, Fred, appeared to be the polar opposite of his wife but he seemed pleasant as he welcomed us from his armchair when he looked up from his book.

"We often make up a foursome and go out with your Mum and Dad," Rita informed us, "It will be nice for Patsy to have children next door to play with, it's been a bit dull round here since the Bradleys moved – there's only little boys, who don't want to play with her, left in the street at the moment."

We spent the rest of the morning in Patsy's bedroom until our father arrived to tell us lunch was ready.

"So you've met Mrs Hopper!" Mum said to us with an obvious wink to Dad. "Quite colourful isn't she!"

"Yes, it must be so difficult to walk on those heels," I said.

"Depends how much practice you've had!" my Mother replied as my father gave a snort of laughter.

"You think she's still carrying on?" he asked.

"What do you reckon!" Flora said as we began to eat, "no smoke without fire!" and the two of them chuckled while we tried to work out what they were talking about.

After lunch the afternoon dragged. We couldn't very well go back to Patsy's house. We didn't know her that well yet. My mother told me to pack up the few things we had brought from home and ensure the two bedrooms were in the same immaculate state as when we arrived, but once that was done there was nothing to do but wait for the sound of Kath's car pulling up outside. The three of us were perched on the edge of the sofa for what seemed like an eternity. Inside my head I was trying to will Kath to arrive. "Please hurry up, please, please hurry up," was going round and round in my brain.

Everyone heard the throb of the engine at the same time. My father opened the front door and we were into the hallway in a heartbeat. I was just about to step past my father into the freedom of fresh air, when my mother's voice shrilled.

"What do you say, Margaret?"

Reddening, I turned to my parents, "Thank you very much for having me," I mumbled, giving Christine and Tina the eye so that they did the same.

"Be good," my mother replied before returning to the lounge as we dashed towards the familiarity of Kath.

When we arrived back in West Street, everything about home had an extra layer of love on it. I looked around our brown front room and welled up with happiness. It was still all there, all the same, with the safety pins on the table ready for a Sunday tea of cockles and muscles. Soon the bread would arrive on its board with the knife, next to Kath, and she would be sitting in grandfather's chair doling out slices and passing the butter, or dripping with salt.

I knew where my parents lived now. It was nice, in an Ideal Home sort of way, but 21A was a real home with its holey lino beneath the threadbare rug and people shouting at one another all day every day. As the kitchen and front room began to fill up with the many aunts and uncles, I sent up a silent prayer that the council wouldn't want to see evidence of our existence too often.

Chapter Eight

On most Friday evenings we were picked up by my father, or Kath would take us over to Hedley Drive. I managed to spend my birthday at home and, when there were occasional friend's parties on a Sunday, I would get out of going then too.

My father generally tried to humour our mother but she was quite childlike in her behaviour and would sulk at the slightest thing. Then he would have to woo her by putting on a silly voice and saying, "Flora! Flora!" she would turn her head and say, "Go away Gerard, go away!", but he would bury his nose in her shoulder and murmur "Now come on, where's my Flora? Where's my little Flora?" until she would start to laugh and it would be all right, for a while.

The one thing that would make him angry was when she went on about money, which she did frequently. They were both in full time employment and not bearing the cost of bringing up their children, but she constantly complained, "Gerard, doesn't give me enough money," and compared him openly with other men they knew.

"Peggy gets so much more from Noel than I get from Gerard, just look at the clothes she has," on and on it would go and we would see our father grinding his teeth in a menacing way. Then he would begin to drum his fingers on the table before his temper oozed out of him from between his gritted teeth.

"Oh for Christ's sake Flora!" and he would drag ferociously on his cigarette.

For the most part, however, they were united in their criticism of other people, more than each other. The times I found most difficult were when we would be all squeezed into the car driving to Peggy and Noel's house and they would mimic the way Mum Williams spoke. Everybody at 21A had pronounced Croydon accents, but my mother did not. My father would regularly give a shout of laughter after saying "Stifficut" like Nell.

"The whole world knows it's 'certific*aaaa*te' except for Nell Williams!"

Nell was the person who cared for me and my sisters constantly throughout our early childhood. For my parents she was an object of derision. I didn't know my mother and father sufficiently well to question the things they were saying, but that in itself made me feel guilty, as if I was colluding against the people I loved and who had shown so much care for me and my sisters.

According to Flora, she had been treated like Cinderella throughout her childhood at 21A. She claimed Kath had been cruel to her, that Hilda was a stirrer and that Marjory was a bitch. Once again, I didn't know what to say or how to react. To nod seemed like agreement, while not saying anything would either make her angry or sulky, or, worse still, encourage further damning accusations in the hope that the weight of "evidence" would crush me into acquiescence.

All I knew was what I had observed. Whenever my mother visited Mum Williams' home it appeared to me as if the sisters were slightly in awe of Flora. Kath often asked her opinion on things, and although my mother certainly wasn't the brightest pebble on the beach, the Williams clan as a whole seemed to think she was a cut above them.

On the question of bringing up their children, Flora and Gerard never deviated from their story. My parents claimed that they had tried on many occasions to reclaim their children, but Mum Williams would not allow them to take us home. They assured us that it was impossible to go against her will, however much they wanted to. I squirmed against this constant maligning of the person, who at that very moment was probably washing and ironing my school uniform so that I would look smart on Monday morning. This was the same elderly lady who would be baking bread for my return the next evening and who, despite her age and constantly painful legs and hands, did everything for me. I wanted no part in the conversation and so I never asked, "if you wanted us so much why didn't you come and visit us regularly?" or, "if you had been unhappy letting one child go, why did you give up a second, and then a third even though they weren't born in Mum Williams' house?"

I didn't say it. But I thought it.

****

As autumn eased into winter Charlie came round to 21A with a threadbare jacket and a torn pair of trousers and we all set to work making our Guy. Cliff donated a pair of scuffed boots with one of the toes out, and we used an old stocking for a head. We then tied up the ends of the sleeves and legs before stuffing the whole thing with newspaper and straw and drawing a grotesque face on the head. A sewn-on mop of black wool for hair completed the look. As the finished gargoyle was loaded onto my go-cart, Kath put her hands on her hips and mused, "You'd get more money if you put Cyril in a chair and wheeled him round the streets," which set Hilda off crying again.

All the kids from the family, plus Philip and his siblings, spent hours trundling our creation around the streets of Croydon calling out "Penny for the Guy", to the indulgent smiles of passers-by and the occasional chink of good fortune when a big round penny landed in our hat.

When I was young we would go to the community bonfire and we would have a few sparklers at home, but once Marjory and Charlie married we used to set fire to their back garden on an annual basis. Cliff and Charlie morphed into complete pyromaniacs and considerably more pennies than we had collected were spent on rockets, roman candles and Catherine wheels.

****

By this time Christine and Tina had finally met Auntie Peggy and Uncle Noel and were as excited about this part of the family as I was.

Uncle Noel always looked very Mediterranean, even in winter, I guess it was the Italian blood. My mother said he could tan in the shade. He and Auntie Peggy used to go to nudist camps and nudist beaches which probably helped, while Peggy was completely upfront about the fact that she never wore underwear wherever she was. Although my mother was enamoured with Noel, all the Bohemianism made her even more nervous and she would never allow Dad to leave the room where she was. If he did, there would be arguments in the car on the way home as she would be convinced he had been talking about her.

"I know you've bin showin' me up," she would say as the sulk began again.

The more I got to know Uncle Noel, the more I admired him. He used to race Jaguars at Silverstone and knew World Champion racing driver, Mike Hawthorn, yet he was also very knowledgeable about history and geology. He was a bit of an inventor, creating hedging lines on a very bad bend on a cliff top in Peacehaven to help stop cars from shooting off the top. These lines are now common on steep bends all over the world. When I first met him he was so quietly spoken and well-mannered that it took me a while to work out how intelligent and influential he actually was. In this respect he was the complete opposite of my Dad who continually talked up his importance and wealth so that it came as a shock to people when they discovered it was mainly hot air.

If Dad drove into a garage with just enough money to buy a gallon of petrol and the attendant asked him which petrol he wanted in his car, he would always choose the most expensive and then go home without a penny in his pocket, rather than opt for a cheaper brand. Gerard wanted to be the big man. Uncle Noel just was.

As the year crept on towards Christmas, Mum Williams had her sewing machine running red hot to make pretty things for my little sisters. The sewing machine was kept in the disused shop, it was one of the old ones with a treadle and I used to hold the material tight for her while she worked. Considering her arthritic legs she still pumped the treadle very fast and I was constantly worried that she would sew right through my fingers, so I tended to wiggle backwards before I should, which led to her exasperated cries of, "Margy, for gawds sake, keep it straight!" but by the time we went carol singing, Mum Williams would have a whole load of stuff made to give to us or her daughters or her poorer neighbours. Anyone she could do a good turn for would have been thought of, with never any expectation that there would be any kind reciprocation for her.

In fact Mum Williams was one of the most difficult people to buy presents for. She was completely content with her life, so she didn't hanker after anything. The only things you could buy her were Turkish Delight, custard tarts or a new flowery pinny.

She always had to have a clean pinny to wear and they usually cost half a crown. If they were any more than that, the shop keeper was a "robbing bastard", so to save her from getting worked up when the cost of pinnies rose to three shillings and sixpence, most of her daughters would buy her new pinnies for Christmas.

We didn't see much of my parents over Christmas, they may have gone to spend time with Peggy and Noel, or had some other excuse with which to appease the neighbours for why we weren't there during the Christmas holidays. When snow and ice made the roads treacherous we were also excused home visits and would be able to take Nell's dustbin lids up Duppas Hill to use as bob sleighs. Many of the kids from my school would be up there and we would be soaked to the bone by the time we dripped our way back through the kitchen door.

"For gawd's sake Margy!" Mum Williams would cry, "Get them things off you before you catch your death."

All my clothes would be hanging in the shop for days as Mum Williams coaxed them to dry and I kept adding to the problem by running out into the street for snowball fights and returning chilled to the marrow again and again. She may have grumbled, but she never really told us off, it was all part of the day's work for Mum Williams and if she didn't have time to tend to us herself, she'd tell Hilda to do it.

By the time spring arrived, our visits to my parents' house were beginning to cause a problem at 21A.

Christine had always been a fussy eater and at Hedley Drive she had been introduced to new luxuries like fish fingers and cornflakes. These sorts of things didn't have a place in our household, for a start we didn't have a freezer. Before we went to school we used to have a full cooked breakfast, or if we were in a hurry it might just be a boiled egg and soldiers. After a few months of weekends at Hedley Drive, Christine began the daily chant of "I don't want that, I want cornflakes!" whenever Mum Williams staggered through from the kitchen with her plate of breakfast.

"Oh shut up and eat yer bacon an' eggs," she'd say as she lumbered out again, while Kath would growl, "that one wants 'er mouth washing out with carbolic, Mum! Get your elbows off the table! Anything left on your plate is what you get at your next meal 'til it's gone. Y' understand? There's no place for yer airs an' graces 'ere!"

Soon Christine would be running from the room, hardly having touched a morsel and Mum Williams would be fretting over whether or not she would become ill. Occasionally Nell became sufficiently worried to buy a box of cornflakes or fish fingers, but that only served to ensure Christine demanded them at every meal and the merry-go-round of refusing, shouting and running off spun more wildly every time.

****

Each Spring Philip would festoon the front room with random jam jars half filled with water and swarming with tadpoles. Unlike his regular collections of grass snakes which would suddenly emerge from various unmarked biscuit tins, I enjoyed helping him with the tadpoles and watching them develop before we carefully returned the tiny frogs to the local ponds where we had found the spawn.

It was just before Easter and the house was unusually quiet. Kath and Mum Williams were banging around in the kitchen as usual, but the front room was empty. I sat at the table surrounded by the jam jars, drawing a birthday card for my mother and trying to understand the adults who surrounded me. I was fighting to work out what was normal and what was not. I already knew from the kids at school that it wasn't normal to live in this house of women rather than with my mother and father. Yet everything that took me away from 21A made me feel frightened and dirty.

I had been round to Mary Nightingale's house earlier in the week. We were helping to lay the table in the kitchen when her father came home. We heard the thump of his bag as he dropped it in the hallway before his deep voice rang out, "Hasn't anyone got a kiss for their hard working Dad!" and Mary dashed towards him, taking a flying leap to put her arms round his neck as he swung her up onto his lap and they collapsed into a chair, laughing. He kissed her forehead and asked her what she had done at school that day.

I smiled at them while a hole of longing and shame seemed to fill my entire chest. "I could never do that with my Dad," I thought. "I would never dare touch my Dad."

Yet he touched me.

It had begun shortly before my tenth birthday. When my mother took my sisters into Croydon to shop on a Saturday morning, I watched them board the bus from the window in the stairwell. As I turned to walk up to the single bedroom I usually stayed in, my father emerged behind me from the bathroom. Roughly twisting my shoulders he pushed me to face the solid banister that ran around the landing. My back was pushed forward over the banister. I smelt his breath. Rasping, guttural sounds were coming from him. For the tiniest moment I thought he was playing a game, but when I twisted my head and saw his contorted face I knew this was nothing frivolous. My body went rigid, and suddenly he dashed into the bathroom and I was left alone to tiptoe into my room.

I felt confused and disgusted. The first time I tried to pretend to myself it hadn't happened. It was an unpleasant dream, about two other people. It wasn't me at all. I had no need to feel afraid.

Mostly it happened at the banister, even if my mother was walking about below us: backwards and forwards between the kitchen and the front door she would go as my eyes begged her to look up and stop what was going on. If she began to climb the stairs my father would quickly push me into a bedroom before going into the toilet.

Sometimes he would go too far. A menacing growl from between gritted teeth would order me to "Go and clean yourself up." Then he would leave as I unbent my stiffened body to mop at the slime that pooled on my back. It looked like the snot that came from some of the boys' noses at school, which they then wiped off in long strings along their sleeves, but I felt a thousand times more revulsion at what was on me.

One moment I would be braced, frozen, at the banister and the next we would all be eating my mother's breaded fish round the dining room table. My Dad would be joking with us, cajoling his family of females to laugh with him and to listen to his stories as he built up his own vision of a hero.

"The things I saw in the war would turn your hair white overnight! If I hadn't gone back for John Joe during the evacuation from Dunkirk I would be without another friend. You never know what a man is capable of until he's staring death in the face ..."

All I would be thinking of would be whether or not Kath would arrive before it happened again. If it was over for another week, or if there was to be more before the big car drew up at the curb.

The previous weekend I had been playing at Patsy's house when there had been a knock. I heard my father's voice as Mrs Harper opened the door.

"Margaret needs to come home now."

"Can't she stay to lunch, I'm just about to serve up."

"No, I've got a present for Flora's birthday and she needs to come and wrap it up while her mother is out."

"All right then. Margaret! Your Dad wants you to go home."

There was no present. It was straight up to the box room.

Sometimes I would wake to find him climbing into my bed smothering us both in a blanket of fear and tension while my mother slept in the next room.

I began to eat. Each layer of fat felt like an extra sliver of armour plating between me and him, and Mum Williams adored feeding me.

****

I loved to laugh and act and sing, but more than this I loved to make other people laugh. It drew them to me, cocooning me within a circle of friends in which, occasionally, I could lose myself and become a child again. Laughter could temporarily obliterate the adult knowledge I was not meant to have and make me feel like a part of normal society again. By now I spent most of my school days feeling exiled from my friends by the inadmissible acts that happened every weekend.

****

At the end of the summer term Mary and I were doing a sketch at the end-of-year show. I was dressed as a boy, but my legs had grown so enormous that the usually baggy shorts were cutting into me as I sang, "There's a hole in my bucket, dear Liza, dear Liza, there's a hole in my bucket, dear Liza, a hole!"

Mary replied with, "Then mend it, dear Henry, dear Henry ..." and the song continued through a range of items with which to fix the bucket. However Uncle Cliff had decided to cut the entire bucket bottom out, so that when I lifted the bucket up to frame my puzzled face the audience collapsed in laughter. I could hear Mary's mother hooting with mirth as she slapped her hands together above her head and whooped for all she was worth. She did everything to make up for the fact that by now Mum Williams' legs were too sore for her to walk up to school functions, and Mrs Nightingale made sure that Nell was told every single detail of any school performance I had taken part in.

The previous Christmas I was meant to have had a very small part in a ballet show. I was the town's ballet elephant. The children were all dressed as robins with brown tights, a hat with a beak and a red satin tummy, which on me was fairly huge. The lead robin should have been danced by a girl named Susan Foster, who went on to become a professional dancer, but she fell ill on the big day. As there was nobody capable of taking Susan's place, I was pushed out on stage first with instructions to do a funny walk using my "wings". Peals of laughter assaulted my vast robin and I was in heaven as I heard Mrs Nightingale laughing like a drain. I imagined her telling Mum Williams, who in turn would tell all the neighbours and the shop keepers, who would all smile indulgently at me, wrapping me safely in their affection.

****

Holidays lasted so much longer as a child and I seemed to do so much in them. The Brownies and the Girl Guides went on camp in East Langdon most summers. This was another activity that involved Nell's family in purchasing a long list of things in addition to my Brownie uniform and the endless proficiency badges that lined both my arms.

Captain Sessions, who ran both troupes, would send home a letter detailing everything that needed to be in my kit bag. I had to have a sleeping bag with a blanket and blanket pins so that it could be made into an inner sleeping bag, plus a tin mug, enamel plate (white and blue) and the Camper's Friend, which was a knife, fork and spoon that all folded in together. We also had a sheath knife each for carving and kindling.

When we arrived on site we first had to dig our latrines in the far corner of the field. We set to work digging a long trench whilst other girls began the endless task of collecting kindling from the woods for our camp fires. Once the trench was deep enough we would erect a set of bamboo poles that were tied together before the canvas was hooked over the back and sides with flaps at the front that could be used as a door. Toilet paper would be hung up on a piece of string and then there would be a spade with some earth at the side of the trench to cover up whatever you had added to the field's fertility. When we broke camp the trench would be completely filled in and covered. We were rigorously instructed on the importance of leaving the field just as we had found it, or better, and we took our ecological duty very seriously.

Daily chores in camp involved carrying water, collecting wood and bathing in the river. Mary and I also did our swimming proficiency badge in the river.

Captain Sessions was a born Guider. It was impossible to imagine her without her Nora Batty stockings, lace-up shoes and a uniform. Her hair was tightly permed and her head held straight and high above a ponderous bust. When we went to camp Captain Sessions would bring along her husband and they would set up their tent a little way away from the rest of us. Naturally, we all imagined their tent was far more luxurious than ours and were perennially curious about what was inside. Mary and I set ourselves up to be "helpful" in our quest to eyeball the interior. Every morning we would take a mug of hot shaving water from the camp fire and stand outside the Sessions' tent.

"Captain Sessions?"

"Yes, who's there?"

"It's Margaret O'Callaghan and Mary Nightingale with the water for Mr Sessions," but each time she would take it through the tent flap without offering so much as a glimpse of their living space.

Once breakfast was over we would be off on excursions armed with our cheese sandwiches. Soon after we bit into the first one, Mr Sessions would say, "Don't eat all the cheese sandwiches girls, save them for the camp fire."

It was so hard to do, but Cheese Dreams – fried cheese sandwiches – were worth the torment of self-control when they were accompanied by camp fire hot chocolate.

There was always plenty of camp fire singing, with Captain Sessions in full voice, and when it grew dark we would start telling ghost stories.

The ten days of camp took me right away, physically and mentally, from my home situation, while the Guides' participation in Church Parade one Sunday a month ensured that on that weekend I could avoid going to Hedley Drive.

At the end of the summer I returned to junior school in the top form. Decked with juvenile responsibilities, my class could enjoy a bit of a strut and swagger as we showed the younger kids how far we had come. There were also our first real exam nerves when we realised we were all soon to take the 11 Plus, our results in this would determine if we ended up at the grammar school or the secondary modern.

Chapter Nine

The final year of primary school was one of preparing for change, for the loss of some friends and beginning on the bottom rung once again. It was also a time of change in Croydon and in Britain as a whole.

Young people were changing. Teenagers were the latest phenomenon as the Teds went on rampages through South London. Wearing velvet-collared jackets, drainpipe trousers and thick-soled shoes with slicked hair-quiffs which took hours of preparation, didn't stop the fashion conscious Teddy Boys from indulging in weekends of pure hooliganism.

My Victorian household stayed the same while a whirlwind of new teenage angst, marches to "Ban the Bomb" and endless leaflets about the Soviet threat jostled to rock our world. Abortion and homosexuality were still illegal; the death penalty was still in force; divorce was shameful and adultery could end your career, even if it had nothing to do with work. The era of drugs and the pill were sweeping down upon a nation that found it easier to pretend nothing was going on than to prepare for what was happening.

At 21A we carried on the same, banging the TV with the flat of our hand to get it to warm up, listening to Kath bait Hilda as she stumbled passed with her teapot, having Cyril thrown out at 10.30pm sharp, all of us living in a house without a bathroom and with an outside privy that would freeze your nether regions most of the year.

Unfortunately another thing that didn't change was my father's behaviour towards me. Although I was so young, I knew about things that set me apart from my friends at school, things I couldn't talk about or even properly explain.

At school it seemed as if I were looking out of windows, not eyes. My friends were living in a world beyond those windows. It was a different world, clean and carefree. On my side of the window there was only dirt and shame. I felt unclean beside their innocence, and, in my mother's pristine house, I felt like filth. Whether it was at the bannister or when he crept into my bed at night, my father took enormous risks. Perhaps my mother knew. I oscillated between wanting her to catch him and make him stop, and knowing that the person who would get into trouble would be me.

It would be my fault. Somehow I was to blame.

I think the confusion became too much for me and I started wetting the bed at Flora's house. The first time it happened I was mortified. I just wanted it to go away. It wasn't my home. There were none of our personal things in this shiny, clean space. There was nothing homely about it at all. I made our beds as usual, but Flora must have smelt it as she stormed down to Mum William's house later.

"She's a dirty little bitch!" she screamed, "wetting my bed in my lovely home! Maybe that sort of repulsive behaviour is acceptable here, but not in my house!"

"That's strange," Mum Williams said slowly as she poured hot water into the pot to make Flora's tea, while keeping the other hand firmly on my shoulder. "Margy's never done that 'ere, not even when she was tiny. It must be a one off. 'ere 'av a nice scone Flora …"

It wasn't a one off, and every time it happened I was terrified of Flora. "What's goin' on Margy?" Mum Williams would ask.

"I can't really tell you," I'd reply and she'd give me an extra squeeze on the shoulder and tell me I'd get used to going to my mother's house soon enough.

One Saturday morning I woke to find myself in a soaking bed once again. I was so scared of Flora that I crept into the bathroom and took her hairdryer in an attempt to dry the sheet and blankets before my shame was discovered. The noise was a giveaway and Flora slapped the back of my legs with all her might, "filthy, filthy bitch!" she screeched yanking the plug out of the wall.

Humiliated in front of my much younger sisters and my family at 21A, I was terrified Auntie Peggy and Uncle Noel would be told. I was out of step with my school friends, feeling soiled, my incontinence was just one more thing I had no control over.

So I ate.

One day, when Mum Williams asked what was going on again, I told her.

"He does things to me."

"The swine!" she said, sitting down heavily beside the kitchen table. I watched her as she sat there looking a little paler than usual. I waited for her solution.

"Ooo, that's shameful, real shameful that is. You must never tell nobody cos your farver will be taken to prison. You wouldn't want that would you? … the swine."

I didn't know if I would want that or not, but I never told.

I think Mum Williams told her daughters – behind a delicate hand in phrases laced with euphemisms. The shame she would have suffered if Gerard had been carted off to Wormwood Scrubs would have been equal to the unhappiness she would have felt from the rift it would have caused between herself and Flora. Better to brush it under the carpet and have a nice cup of tea.

I still went to Flora's house most weekends but I did get times off when I would enjoy the normal family Friday evenings and maybe walk over Duppus Hill with Ivy and Cliff to stay with them. My little garden bedroom at their house seemed even more peaceful in the light of what I was experiencing at my parents place in Hedley Drive. The morning sun would stream through Ivy's curtains as the starlings hopped on the lawn and the trees were full of bird song. I was warm, comfortable, safe. I felt clean.

****

On the weekends when I was allowed to stay at 21A I would often be sent to pay Marjory's debts. Hire purchase, or "the never-never" as it was known, had just been invented and Marjory found it irresistible. She was driven to "keep up with the Joneses" and then terrified that Charlie might find out.

To cover her tracks Mum Williams used to go into their house every day while they were at work and remove any incriminating mail. Then at our Friday evening gathering Marjory would sneak me a fistful of little cards and more money than I would usually see in our home in a month of Sundays. It would take me several hours to go round to all the stores and get each one stamped "paid" with the date on it.

****

May Day had come round again and the sisters had the annual whip round for our white socks and buck skin sandals. Our hair was curled, our head-dresses made and we were enjoying a weekend in the arms of our community. That year our church colours were white dresses with burgundy cummerbunds and matching flowers.

We had done our round of singing at the old people's homes and been to the church to get blessed. We had danced round the maypole with gusto, weaving our ribbons in and out to dress the pole and despite my rotund legs and tummy I had skipped happily with all the rest of the children. An almost carefree ten-year-old. Almost still a child.

Our May Day tea was in the community hall at the back of the secondary school. After feasting, we normally played in the hall until the prizes were awarded for the best dressed May Queen and King. I went to the toilet and found my knickers full of blood. Mary Nightingale was in the next cubicle.

"Quick, go and get my Auntie Ivy," I called out, knowing that Ivy was in the hall.

"Why?"

"Just go and get her, please!" Mary scampered off and within minutes Ivy was knocking on the toilet door.

"Margy, let me in, let me in …"

"I'm bleeding, I've got blood everywhere."

"Where's your coat?"

I sent her out to the coat rack for my navy blue school coat that looked like everybody elses – only bigger!

"Come on, quick." Ivy marched me across the road in a way that made me slightly less certain I was dying. With an urgent whisper to Mum Williams I was propelled into the kitchen and the door was firmly shut.

Helping me to remove my pristine white dress and soggy knickers, Mum Williams started to clean me with a bowl of water before producing a belt with what looked like a hammock slung between it. She then took my hand and led me into the outside privy before putting it on me and announcing, "You're going to get this every month now. Don't tell any boys."

That was it. No more information. No sudden death either, which was a relief.

Luckily my period didn't reappear again until I was 15 by which time other girls in my class had provided some insight on the matter. Sex "education" was a rather hit or miss affair, at 21A they thought you could catch gonorrhoea by reading the same newspaper as someone who had it. My school friends believed you could get pregnant by kissing. Information before Google could be exceedingly confusing!

The date for my Eleven Plus exam was fast approaching and I was a bundle of nerves. Whether or not you passed this exam signified which school you were sent to – the grammar school, the high school or the secondary modern. Everyone had to take it, but for me, with everything else that was happening around me, it seemed overwhelming.

One day before the exam my whole body was covered in an angry rash. Hilda was instructed to take me into the doctor while Mum Williams skulked outside trying to avoid any nurses or other medical personnel who might attempt to cajole her into seeing a doctor herself.

"What's 'e say? Did 'e give you a stifficut?" she asked the moment Hilda and I exited.

"Says it might be shingles and to keep 'er 'ome an' bring 'er back next week if it's not better."

Directly the exam was over, it cleared up immediately, so I ended up taking my Eleven Plus in the school hall with one other pupil a week later. There was never much question that I would be going to the school directly across the road from 21A, but now it was official. It would be a new start. A new set of children I would feel older than, whilst desperately trying to join in their childish games. A new set of people to amuse, to find out what made them laugh and use it every way I could.

Before I started at my new school, however, some of the things I had learnt at Girl Guides were unexpectedly useful. As usual there were a bunch of children and babies stacked into 21A. I was left in charge of Christine, Tina, Marjory's twins Trevor and Jaqueline plus a couple of babies in prams in the living room. Mum Williams had just taken the dinner she had made for Marjory's family out of the gas oven. It was a chilly evening and, as the menfolk had stopped Mum Williams from using the range, there was a paraffin heater alight in the kitchen. As Mum Williams went out of the back door with the casserole for Marjory, a gust of wind caught the big piece of chipboard which had been propped up to block the range. It slammed down on the paraffin heater spilling liquid paraffin all over the floor and with one whoosh the kitchen was engulfed in flames. Dragging the older children out of the main door I ran back and fought with the pram brakes to manoeuver them out of the house as well. By the time they were all safely on the hard standing the fire had completely taken hold. I ran across to the fire station and rang the bell like my life depended on it, as I'd been shown to do when I took my fire badge at the station only a couple of months before.

The fire truck was at 21A incredibly quickly but it was still too late for Kath's dog which had been asleep under the kitchen table. Once we were allowed back inside the house, I sat shaking uncontrollably in Hilda's chair.

Sub-Officer Louis came and squatted in front of me, "What do we do next Margy?" he said with a gentle smile.

"I don't know! I don't know!" I said, completely panicked.

"We have to make a cup of tea!" he growled with an exaggerated wink, "give me that badge back if you can't remember the most important part!"

Chapter Ten

Do the long lazy summers of childhood seem like never-ending tastes of paradise in everyone's memories? Despite her age, I think Mum Williams enjoyed those bright warm days as much as we did. She spent her life gaining pleasure from her daughters and all the other children who surrounded her.

Nell was now over seventy and her arthritis was frequently terrible, but the balmy summer weather would give her a little respite from the pain and she would take the five of us – me and my sisters plus Trevor and Jacqueline – blackberry picking in Elswood. Even with Kath driving us, it was a major undertaking involving piles of sandwiches and pies and then a whole load more cooking of the blackberries themselves when we got back. After filling every container we had, and getting black around our fingers and mouths in the process, we would stop off at Elswood pub on the way home where there were swings and a slide. Mum Williams would buy us glasses of pop while she and Kath enjoyed a shandy as the final sandwiches were polished off.

There were summer picnics, Guide camp and extra pocket money when I did errands for the grocer's shop opposite our house. I would earn thruppence an errand plus the odd broken biscuit if I was lucky.

Ivy's husband, Cliff, made the most of the summer too. He would have been a brilliant Dad but in the absence of his own children he employed us to fill the gap. Our morning slumber would frequently be shattered by Cliff ringing a bell in our ears, "Come on, it's a perfect day, let's have a run down to the beach!", or "There's a breeze that's great for flying kites, let's get down to Epsom Downs!" Whatever idea he had, he would get everyone out of bed and packed into the car before they'd rinsed the sleep out of their eyes. Cliff would be first in the sea whilst everyone else was shivering on the tideline, splashing us until we got in and played.

Charlie was good at joining in as well, but sometimes Marjory would prefer to be a little more sedate than the menfolk, although her efforts at elegance didn't work too well on the day she opted to stay standing at the rails along the promenade while we flew our kites on Brighton beach. As she attempted to lean gracefully against the railings a dog came along and peed all down her leg.

"I told you, you 'ad legs like tree trunks!" Charlie said giving her a friendly punch as she tried to clean off in the sea. With all of Mum William's cooking none of us were going to give Twiggy anything to worry about!

Although Marjory and Charlie had their own twins they would sometimes take one of us on holiday with them. In my last year of junior school it was Christine's turn and they were off for a week at a caravan park. On the way there Charlie's car broke down and the garage that fixed it cost them all their holiday money. They had sufficient for the caravan but nothing for anything else. Rather than come home, they phoned Mum Williams and asked her to send a postal order, which arrived two or three days later.

"'Ow did the five of you survive wiv-out a penny for three days?" Mum Williams asked.

"Our caravan was just in front of a potato field so once it was dark we went and dug up enough potatoes to feed us the next day," Marjory said. "There aint nothin' I can't do with a potato now! I chipped them, boiled them, put them in milk, made omelettes with 'em, 'ad them in jackets, absolootly everythin'!"

****

Mary Nightingale was going to the High School rather than the Secondary Modern with me, so I was going to have to make new friends in September. Although I had experienced several eye operations by now, I still had "one eye in the pot and the other up the chimney", also my weight was substantial and I knew that my new companions were likely to live with their mums and dads, usually in houses that had bathrooms. All the differences weren't a good start to fitting in at a new school.

It may sound melodramatic, but for most of my school life I wished my parents were dead. It would have been so much easier to explain.

"Where do you live?"

"Across the road." Then someone would chip in with, "she lives with the old witch in the corner ..."

Mum Williams' long grey hair, facial birthmark and crooked nose led some children to be cruel, but to me she was the most kind loving "mother" in the world.

"That's my Nan, she's not a witch!"

"Why don't you live with your mum and dad?"

"I go there at weekends."

"Do they live a long way away?"

"No."

"So why don't you live with them instead of the witch?"

You get the picture. As ever, "the witch" and her daughters took incredibly good care of me. Every break time Hilda would come across the street with rock cakes or sandwiches and milk.

Despite the difficulties of explaining my home situation, I loved my new school. It was attached to the church so we had a mixture of Church of England nuns and regular teachers. Every day began with a long religious service, including a pertinent lesson, and our timetable contained an inordinate number of Religious Knowledge classes. Every saint's day or other church festival would see a crocodile of all the children marching across to St. Andrew's to ensure it was properly celebrated.

I was good at all my new academic studies but cookery and needlework left me bored to tears. Luckily I had a partner in boredom, Marilyn McCardle. She made the taunts of my classmates far easier to bear.

While Dawn Spence and Avril French would be putting the finishing stitches into beautiful aprons and skirts, which they would flourish in front of us, Marilyn and I would spend the entire lesson praying for the bell to go. Sister Cornelius would do her best to inspire us by enthusing about the new materials that had arrived, but in the four years I was there both Marilyn and I failed to finish the first assignment which was to make a huge envelope in which to put all our future work!

The envelope was supposed to be half a metre wide with a "V" that fastened with a popper and with our name embroidered in chain stitch on the front, but we spent most of the time chatting and unpicking the mess we had made during the previous lesson.

Cookery was slightly better, mainly because Marilyn and I had a plan. When we had finished making unidentifiable blobs, there would be a list of jobs that needed doing.

"Volunteers for cleaning the ovens ..." and two classmates would shoot up their hands, whilst we sat firmly on ours.

"... volunteers for wiping down the tops ..." still sitting.

"volunteers for clearing up the store room ..." we'd be almost leaping out of our seats, "Me miss, please me!"

Our idea of "clearing up" was perhaps slightly unconventional as it involved slipping the odd egg into our apron pockets, plus a bit of sugar, a twist of flour and anything else that looked useful. When I arrived home and handed it all to Mum Williams she'd be cursing me for being a "little thief" whilst asking me "What else did you get then?" and if I had been particularly dexterous she'd call out to Kath, "Eh, look at this, there's enough for a nice sponge for Sunday tea!"

Sunday tea was my time to breathe easy again. If I had been to my parents' house it was the time when it was over for at least another week. Friday afternoons were the polar opposites to Sunday tea for me.

My classmates relished the idea of the weekends while, for the most part, I dreaded them. Despite my frozen rigidity whenever he touched me, I don't think my father had any idea how I felt about his actions and how much I longed for a normal father figure. One day when he picked the three of us up from 21A, I was in the front seat and my sisters were in the back. The traffic lights turned to red in Coombe Road while my father was in the middle of one of his tirades about how selfish and chippy Flora was. He often let vent to us about how he hated her sulkiness and extravagance.

Then he turned to me with a benevolent smile, the brown stained fingers of his hand reaching out to squeeze my knee, "At least I've got you my little princess, my Cleopatra ..."

It was going to be a long weekend.

Our visits to Hedley Drive didn't just cause problems for me, however, by now processed cheese, Wonderloaf, Heinz Tomato Soup and Spaghetti in tins had been added to the national diet together with the breakfast cereal and fish fingers that had already caused so much trouble. Christine became increasingly averse to Mum Williams' cooking, and she was getting taller.

If we didn't eat everything that Mum Williams had put on our plates, which were carefully brought in one at a time, her two thumbs lapped by the deep pool of gravy, then the remainder would be served up at the next meal.

"We 'aven't got money to burn" was the retort to anyone who didn't want to eat it all, followed by, "go on, I've done it all nice f' you."

Despite her good intentions there was no finesse with Mum Williams' cooking. It would frequently involve steak and kidney pudding followed by spotted dick! Christine wanted finesse. When she saw Mum Williams swaying towards her with a plate she didn't fancy she would leap down from the sitting board and wallop Nell across her back as she dashed out of the room. The force could literally rock Mum Williams off her feet and so I would dash after Christine, intent on teaching her a lesson not to upset my beloved Nan. Of course, as the two of us were careering around the house the meal time descended into its usual round of shouts, screams and rants. For me it was homely heaven. But Christine hated it.

However, being the only one with dark hair like my father, she was also the only one who was never touched, so I guess she had a totally different perspective on her parents and the possibilities of an idyllic life at Hedley Drive.

****

The most important part of the curriculum for me at my new school was music. My teachers, Brian Knight and Molly Milbank were both part of the London Symphony Choral Society and they infected me with their enthusiasm for all things musical. I had always sung, in the church choir, in the Girl Guides concerts and at my junior school, so I automatically got into the secondary school choir, but my musical education took quantum leaps when we went to see Madame Butterfly, Tosca and La Bohème.

I discovered that I not only loved Cliff Richard, but also Puccini, Mendelssohn and Mozart. Music became the way I kept in touch with my soul.

I was different and I knew I was different, but music allowed me to escape. It spoke to parts of me that I could never explain. It became my passion and as my teachers saw they had a protégé I was encouraged daily to sing more, listen more, experience more. My life took on a new love, one that was completely private, a love that only I knew how much it moved me and how much I needed it.

Chapter Eleven

Speed and wheels, the things I had always coveted, were becoming realities. Whenever we went to camping with the family, Charlie would let me drive his car around the site although I was only 12 or 13. I was mad keen to get on the road.

Philip, being six years older than me, had already got himself a motorbike. He was so indulgent of me, appearing most lunch times to take me out on the back of his shiny new machine. Mum Williams was constantly worried about accidents, but she didn't stop me from going and I relished the wind whipping through my hair as we leaned violently round corners, Croydon's couple of midday speed junkies.

I had also acquired a more sedate set of wheels for myself in the form of a Raleigh 26" bicycle with a big front bag so that I could do a paper round every morning. With my thruppence an errand from the grocer and becoming the paper girl for West Street, Queens Street and Lord Street, I was getting to be quite the entrepreneur. I was given the morning paper round for an initial three months, after that time I would have to take on an evening round so that all the kids who wanted to work got a chance at the popular morning spot.

Everybody was up and about early in those days. The milk floats were out on the street, as was the baker's van and the paper boys and girls. There seemed to be a great deal of time before school and we used to do lots of activities. Christine and Tina would be colouring up at the table before Mum Williams came in with the cooked breakfasts, the Hilda and Kath would be dispatched to the bakers or the greengrocers to ensure Mum Williams had everything she needed to cook for the day, and I would be off with my bag stuffed with the day's newspapers waving to all my neighbours as I shot past them on my mean machine.

For a while Mum Williams took Friday nights off from cooking mountains of food and would ask me to "go get us some fish and chips on yer bike."

Unfortunately I was swiftly sacked from this job because I could not resist making a hole in the newspaper and dibbing into the bag as I cycled home, eating most of the chips on the way.

"Look at the number of chips 'e's given us for all that money!" Mum Williams protested. "e's short changed me, the robbing bastard, you get down the phone box 'ilda and tell 'im I want a refund!"

I had to own up. I wasn't sent again.

Unfortunately the evening paper round was too much for Mum Williams. She didn't mind me being out early but once it was dark, and getting darker, she worried.

"What about if you come a cropper in the dark and nobody sees you?" she fretted. "I'm not 'appy, not 'appy at all …" and if Mum Williams wasn't happy, things tended to change quite swiftly.

However, everybody was happy about my performance at school. Despite the wonky eye I was excelling at almost everything, including netball. I became the school team's shooter, carefully measuring the distance up with my one good eye, tongue out in concentration, scoring goals almost every time.

Soon afterwards I became netball team captain, in charge of the bands we wore – although I was so big I had to wear the band that held all the others together! Sister Cornelius, my long-suffering needlework teacher, couldn't reconcile my size with physical activity and one day when I was enjoying a particularly vigorous game, she opened the window at the top of the school and bellowed across the playground, "Stop that girl! Get that girl off the playground! She's so fat she's going to have a heart attack!"

We all stopped and I felt completely crushed. Our games teacher, Miss Rogers, was so skinny you'd find more fat on a crisp. As usual she was on the pitch in her shorts, white blouse and high heeled shoes tottering around with her whistle. For one long moment she looked up at Sister Cornelius, then she put her whistle to her mouth, blew it with all her might and yelled, "Play on girls!"

I never knew if she said anything to the nun, but like some of the other fat-related incidents, it stuck in my mind.

****

When I was 13 the school announced they would be organising a ski-ing trip to Switzerland. By this time I was old enough to recognise all the sacrifices Mum Williams and her daughters had made for me over the years and I honestly did not want them to make any more, so I didn't take the letter home. There was no way they could have afforded the trip, let alone the outfits that would have been necessary, but if the letter had gone home they would have felt duty bound to do so.

Everything was going swimmingly until Mrs Frith stopped to chat at the gate one day. "Is your Margaret going on the school trip?" she enquired.

"'Ere, what's all this about Dorothy Frith going on a school trip I don't know nothin' about? Why didn't you bring the letter 'ome?" was her greeting as I crashed through the door that afternoon.

I couldn't say the real reason so I attempted to improvise, "There wasn't a letter, you had to be chosen, and I wasn't chosen …"

"Well that's not right," she said, hobbling to the coat hook and shrugging on her gabardine. "I'm not 'avin' none of that, you're as good as Dorothy Frith, there's no reason why you can't go on no foreign trip …"

"No, really Mum, it's fine, I don't want to go."

"That's not the point, they're not givin' you the hopportunity, it's not right, I'm goin' up there right now to give 'em a piece of my mind. They can't be putting the likes of Dorothy Frith above you."

"No Mum, I just wasn't chosen," I was beginning to cry.

"What the 'ell's the matter wiv you? Takin' on like this," she said as I fished my hankie out of my knickers to dry my tears.

"I really don't want you to go up to the school!" I cried

"Why the 'ell not? I'm telling you it's not right to choose between one child and anover, they need tellin'!"

"Please Mum, please don't, I didn't get chosen but I was happy about it because I DON'T WANT TO GO!"

"Yes, but you ought't 'av 'ad the chance …"

"But if you go up there then they might give me the chance, and I don't want to go!"

"I think I should 'ave a word …"

"Please, please don't!" Slowly she began removing her coat.

"I still think I ought t' tell 'em …"

"Maybe if it happens again, and I want to go," I wheedled, "But for now, let's just have a nice cup of tea."

****

It was Friday morning and I was feeling sick and apprehensive. We were studying Rudyard Kipling in our English Literature lesson, the poem of The Smuggler's Song to be exact. I felt as if I were squirming in my seat, as if we were reading this poem just because I was in the class, that they all knew I was dirty - that they could read it in my face.

It's a poem about letting men do what they want while the women keep quiet. It didn't matter that it was about smugglers, as far as I was concerned it was about me.

"…You be careful what you say, and mindful what is said."

"… If you do as you've been told, 'likely there's a chance, You'll be give a dainty doll, all the way from France …"

"Them that asks no questions isn't told a lie – Watch the wall my darling while the Gentlemen go by!"

It was the last phrase that really haunted me. Leaning over the bannister I would watch the opposite wall every weekend, and the man behind me would certainly believe that "gentlemen" should always be written with a capital "G".

He would go to great lengths to keep me in the house. Often my mother would want to go to Croydon to shop on a Saturday morning and the three of us would say, "Can we come with you?" Immediately, my father would interrupt, "I need Margaret to help me, but you can take the two little ones." I would stand at the upstairs window watching as they went down the road, thinking "is there still a chance I can go? Are they at the bus stop yet? Has the bus come?" but the "Gentleman" would come up behind me and there would be no escape from my feelings of revulsion and filth.

Nobody talked about it. All I could do was pray for a weekend off. The wedge of knowledge between me and my school friends seemed to get bigger every day.

****

I escaped. Every time I sang my mind became whole clean and clear again. It was my release. I was the school's star soloist so when we were booked to sing at Fairfield Halls, soon after it was opened by the Queen Mother, I was chosen to sing Mendelssohn's *Wings of Song*. As a choir we sang parts of Handel's *Messiah*, and I also sang a duet of Schubert's *The Trout*.

Fairfields Hall had been built as an exact replica of the Festival Hall in London with a stage, orchestra pit and choir stalls, there were cones in the ceiling for acoustics and on the night I was performing the full audience included Sir Malcolm Sergeant, Ivy and Marjory – Mum William's legs were too bad to come that far – all dressed in their most elaborate finery.

Whilst I was a nervous pupil if I was questioned in front of the class at school about something academic, I had no qualms at all when I was singing on stage; it was as natural to me as breathing.

This wasn't the only big concert we gave. Molly Millbank and Brian Knight were so well up in the London Symphony Choral Society that we ended up at the Albert Hall at the inter-schools competition. We rehearsed for months beforehand. I couldn't get enough of it. The choir, in freshly pressed school uniforms, went up to London on a bus and then we were packed into a round dressing room to do our breathing exercises.

I couldn't wait to get out there. Walking into the wings I saw how vast the stage was. Every seat was taken, but I strode out there full of confidence as Brian Knight lifted his baton and we hit the first notes of the *Hallelujah Chorus*.

Soon after this Brian Knight, Molly Millbank and the Headmaster walked across the road to see Mum Williams. She welcomed them into the front room and instantly plied them with tea and cake, although she was clearly in a bit of a flurry about the unexpected visit of two such eminent gentlemen.

"Margy's been doin' alright at 'er studies 'asn't she?"

"She most certainly has," the Headmaster said, smiling broadly. "She won the science prize this term, but what we are here for is to talk to you about her music."

"Mrs Williams, we want to ask you if you would mind if we sent out application forms in Margaret's names to some of the music colleges," Brian Knight took over the explanations. "Her singing ability is so good we are certain she could gain a scholarship and we would give her all our backing every step of the way."

Mum Williams was visibly swelling with pride and I was bursting with so much happiness I could hardly sit still in my seat. I had to put my teacup down because my hands were shaking so much.

"She's the best music student I've had the privilege to teach at St Andrews," Molly Millbank added quietly. I reckoned I had died and gone to heaven! Music College would not only be my ultimate dream but it would take me far away from my parents and make Mum Williams as proud as punch.

"Well, of course," Mum Williams gushed, fumbling with the tea pot, "If the three of you fink our Margy should go to college, then she should go! So long as you don't forget where your 'ome is," she said giving me a squeeze on my shoulder as my eyes brimmed with happiness. I could already taste the feeling of striding out onto every London stage and hitting top C. Days didn't come any better than this. The smile was tattooed onto my face even while I slept. I was going to music college. Music was going to be my life.

Chapter twelve

"Oh no, Gerard and I won't be 'aving none of that. We've already discussed it. Margaret will leave school now. We need 'er home to get a job and pay 'er way." My mother had come for a cup of tea a week or so after the Headmaster's visit and Mum Williams had been proudly telling her the content of their recent conversation.

"But she's not 15 'til September. College wouldn't take too long and if she got a scholarship it wouldn't cost nuffin', they was so proud of 'er, she could be a star! She's such a credit to you Flora."

"Rubbish, it's Christine who 'as the brains of the family, Gerard's always saying so. Margaret is coming to live with us at the end of this term, Gerard's already got 'er a job lined up at a garage. She's to start in July and goodness knows we could do with the money! Gerard keeps me that short … compared to what Peggy gets from Noel I have the life of a pauper from the gutter!"

"Oh dear Flora, is it that bad? You sit yourself down and I'll get you a cuppa and a fresh scone with jam, just 'ow you likes it."

I would be leaving school within a month. I loved my school. All the dreams had been painted inside my head, but my mother had come for an hour and thrown acid on them. The teachers didn't try to dissuade my parents because they didn't know them. They had never met them. I was the only child in my class leaving school. All my friends were staying on until they were 15 or 16, even the ones with zero aptitude for any studies. Plus I was to live in my parents' cold, dangerous house and make money for them at whatever job my father had lined up for me. I found it almost impossible to stop crying.

Christine was delighted. "If you're going to live at Hedley Drive, I'm going to live there too." As my candle of hope was snuffed out, my nine-year-old sister discovered utopia; a life far away from the mealtime shouting, or the snivelling Hilda whenever Kath had a go at her as she exited from the cellar. Christine would be living in a shiny house with fish fingers and cornflakes, where there were candlewick bedspreads on the beds instead of piles of coats. Flora may have anticipated having one, useful, child home, but Christine was completely determined she was going to get two.

Brian Knight tried to remain an impartial teacher but he was clearly upset that his plans for his protégé had been so completely stamped upon. My mother's announcement happened at the end of May. During the final month I was at St Andrew's Brian Knight would regularly tiptoe into my classes and ask to take me to the library where the big tape recorder was kept.

"I want to record you singing *The Trout*," he would say, or, "Do you remember when you sang *Wings of Song* at Fairfields? Can you sing it like that again for me to record?"

His enthusiasm to capture my voice before it was lost in a Croydon motor garage made me feel special. It cemented the feeling that there was one thing I had real talent for whether or not my parents could appreciate it.

"You must join the Croydon Operatic and Dramatic Association", Molly Millbank said, "It would be terrible to let your music go just because you've left school. I'll put a word in with the principal."

Philip was kind to me too. Although he was 20 by now he knew how upset I was and tried to cheer me up by bringing over his record player and teaching me to jive. The rest of the family put up with all the furniture being rearranged against the walls of the front room as Cliff Richard's *Living Doll* blasted out and we jived for all we were worth. During the last week of my life at 21A Philip announced he was taking me out. "Be ready by 5.30 and I'll pick you up on the bike."

Mum Williams was invigilating my every move as I combed my hair before the front room mirror.

"I 'ope you don't think you're putting on none of that lipstick! I'm not 'aving a girl of mine goin' out with any of that muck on 'er face!"

"I wouldn't dream of it Mum!" I muttered as I threw my school coat over my best dress.

Philip had been more thoughtful than I could have imagined. He took me to see Disney's *Fantastia*. I was swept up in the music, the colours and the stories. Like the opera, it was something I could truly lose myself in. Music may have made me cry, regularly, but they were tears of catharsis, not the frustrated angry sobbing I descended into every time I thought of my torpedoed college career.

****

I managed to side-step my father's first garage job by getting myself a position as an apprentice window dresser at a dress shop in Croydon.

We were leaving Hedley Drive in plenty of time as my father had to drop Christine at school and Flora and myself at work. I had got up early to make sure I looked my best for my first day in the shop but nevertheless I was quite nervous. Christine and I were sitting in the back seat of the car and Gerard had the motor running but my mother continued to be absent.

"Oh for Christ's sake, where's Flora? Margaret, go and see where your mother is!"

I found my mother lying in a pool of blood at the bottom of the stairs. She had tripped on her way down and sliced her head open on the tiled window sill. We drove like crazy to Croydon General and luckily the injury looked far worse than it was. There were no mobile phones, no way to tell the shop what had occurred, so I arrived the following morning and explained the situation, but they said, "Sorry, you didn't turn up so we can't take you on." End of story. Back to Gerard's jobs.

The following day my father got me a job in a car spare parts warehouse called Edmunds & Walker. Mechanics would come in and ask for a box of this or one of those. All the girls were upstairs in the office filling in the huge accounts ledgers and ordering whatever stock was needed. I was the office junior, the lowest of the low, merely allowed to handle the stamp book, make tea and do the filing. It was a bitchy place and the biggest bitch was a girl called Anne who used to wear her hair in a beehive with massive make-up like Amy Winehouse. She would totter around on stiletto heels with winkle picker toes and would go to any lengths to get me into trouble. I hated it, so I left.

The old man instantly got me another job, still in the motor trade. I turned up and the boss said, "You're Gerry's daughter," and when I confirmed it he said "All I want you to do is answer the phone, make the tea and do errands."

There was one other lady at the garage but she was in the cashier's office which was up a wooden staircase, so I never got to chat with her. I was parked in a tiny cupboard just at the side of the garage. All the men who worked there hated the boss. Whenever I began to go round with the tray of teas they'd say, "Which one's 'is?" then one of them would take it off to the toilet and pee in it. So I left there too.

I used to cry most nights and I was constantly angry with my mother - ferociously angry.

"I don't know why you're so down in the dumps the 'ole time!" Flora would complain as I glowered at her, "We give you a lovely 'ome and all you do is act all miserable, you don't know when you've got it good!" She didn't seem to have a clue, or she didn't want to have one.

Every day Gerard would do the rounds to drop Christine at school before dropping Flora and I off at our respective work places. Tina would walk to school from Mum William's house. Christine and Tina were only 18 months apart in age and attended the same school, the situation was exceedingly weird.

I went back to 21A at every opportunity I could. There was always the same lovely feeling of home when I pushed open the door and stepped from the hall onto the threadbare carpet in the front room. It smelt of home. It was the place I would always find a genuine smile. It might be loud and chaotic, but it was my type of noise and my type of chaos, a chaos I could laugh about and enjoy.

After the tea-pee job, Gerard was proposing I start work at another friend's garage.

"Every job he sends me to is awful," I said to Mum Williams over a cup of tea and a couple of custard tarts I had bought for her on my way through town. "It's not that I can't do the work, but the type of people who are employed there are gross!"

"You can't carry on in them disgustin' places," Mum Williams agreed, "Let's 'av a look in the paper."

By chance we discovered that Hamleys were advertising for an assistant in the doll department. We clipped the advert out of the paper and I went into Croydon the next morning to apply. The shop was owned by Cedric Hamley, the disowned brother of Hamley's in London. As he used the same name, everyone associated his store with the huge toy emporium in the City even though it was nothing to do with the Croydon shop at all.

The shop was very old and on three floors with Cedric Hamley's office at the very top. I got the job. It was great. My manageress was a German lady called Mrs Stone. Every day we had to make sure that the dresses on the dolls were not crinkled and that the dolls eyes were properly open, so we would open all the big cabinets and ensure each one of them looked lovely.

At the end of my first week I walked down to 21A to tell Mum Williams all about it. I was starving but I didn't want Mum to go to any trouble so I stopped at Coughlin's Bakers and bought a pie. They made every type of pie: chicken and mushroom, apple, steak and kidney, ham and leek ...

"I'll have a steak and kidney, please."

Obviously Mum Williams had no idea I was coming straight from work but she was so pleased to see me, "Oh gawd, 'ello! Do you want somefin' t'eat?" before I had even got through the door!

"I've got a pie Mum, so please don't worry …"

"I'll cook you some chips with that, and put the pie to warm in the oven, it won't take me no time to do you some chips … I'll make you a cuppa tea … go on, you sit down…" she said hobbling about on her arthritic bandy legs while cutting up the potatoes. It was exactly what I wanted to avoid happening, but there was no stopping her and she was as happy as a summer's day despite her obvious physical pain. "I'll 'av t'get it all done before Kath comes because you know what she's like with all the fat spitting. 'Ere you are, d'you want some sauce on that, or I could do you some gravy …"

"Just some brown sauce please Mum."

"I'll do it in the kitchen, I won't put the sauce on the table," so she covered the plate in brown sauce and brought it out. "What about salt and vinegar?"

"Just some salt Mum," I said, feeling increasingly desperate that she should sit down so we could actually have a chat. So she took the plate out again and covered it in salt. Finally I cut into my pie. It was cherry.

Once again the plate was whisked away. She gave the pie a bit of a shake and a bit of a scrape and set it aside.

"I'll cut you some bread 'n' butter, you can 'av some chip butties. I'll 'av that pie later with a cuppa tea. I'll enjoy that!"

No waste at 21A!

****

Now that I had a proper job Flora told me I should go and buy furniture for my room. Up to this point there had just been a bed and I was making do as well as I could. I went to a company called Leebus and bought a combination wardrobe with drawers underneath and a mirror set in for a little dressing table. I paid for it weekly on hire purchase and was rather proud of my first major acquisition, it all fitted perfectly into the box room over the stairs.

I was doing well at Hamleys and happily stayed behind to help with stock taking. Eventually I was summoned up to the office of Mr Cedric. He looked at me over the top of his glasses, "I'm very pleased with you, and Mrs Stone is very pleased with you too." I stood there, smiling happily but he dropped his eyes and mumbled, "you can go, you can go …"

"How did you get on?" Mrs Stone asked in hushed tones as I came back downstairs.

"He says he's very pleased with me."

"Did he give you a rise?"

"No"

"Oh, I thought he'd give you a rise, you ought to ask."

"I can't!" my 15-year-old-self was terrified at the idea of asking the boss for money.

The next day Mrs Stone was insistent, "go on, up you go and see Mr Hamley."

So I climbed back up the stairs and knocked on his door. "Come in! Oh, it's you!" I stood with my hands behind my back so that he couldn't see that they were trembling.

"Scuse me Mr Hamley, but I was wondering if it's possible to have a rise."

"A rise?" he said, his voice becoming unnecessarily loud, "You mean an increment in your wages?"

"Yes please, my bus fare's gone up and it's now costin' me a shillin'." He didn't look angry, but he didn't say anything either, just waved me away and I clattered downstairs to await my fate.

That week he gave me a shilling more and put it into my wage packet, all in pennies. He touched me on the shoulder when he came to pay everybody, "There's a little something extra my dear in your wage packet this week!" I was earning two pounds and 10 shillings, so an extra shilling was quite a big deal. I was delighted, and sufficiently canny to know I shouldn't breathe a word of it to Flora!

After Flora and Gerard had taken their cut, I was left with a pound and a few shillings for myself each week. As I left work every Friday with my wage packet stashed in my handbag I would jump on the bus and head straight for Mum Williams' house, getting off at the cobbled passageway that led down to Queens Street and walking on to where we lived. I always got off the bus early because I liked to spend my extra pound on extravagant groceries for the family who had given me so much – and with whom my youngest sister still lived.

I would stop at United Dairies and buy cheese, eggs, butter, milk, packets of tea, Fray Bentos Steak and Kidney pies in tins and custard tarts. Mum Williams didn't have teeth but she loved custard tarts and if I ever had an afternoon off I would buy four of them and together we would sit in front of the fire and gorge ourselves. Whenever I took in my Friday bag of groceries, Mum would squeak with delight while protesting.

"Aww Margy, you can't do this, what are you like! Oh Kath look, look what we've got 'ere, look what she's done!" All the family would gather round and go through the bag as if it were gold, frankincense and myrrh. I felt ten feet tall!

Kath adored Fray Bentos pies and whenever I arrived with one she'd grab it saying, "Oh I'll love that, Mum, with a bit of mashed potato!" It was such a pleasure to feel as if I was finally giving something back.

We would ease into the Friday evening rituals, analysing the local paper, Kath's port and arrowroot biscuit, dissecting the week that had gone. It was the time of the Cuban missile crisis and the world was holding its collective breath as the superpowers teetered on the brink of nuclear war – all of the world, that is, apart from the occupants of 21A.

There were plenty of Ban-the-Bomb marches and people had begun camping out on Greenham Common in protest. We would receive regular advice leaflets through the post-box, one was entitled "Advising the Householder on Protection Against Nuclear Attack" and included useful information such as: "If you have to go outside in a nuclear attack, put on gumboots or stout shoes … a hat or headscarf, coat done up to the neck, and gloves." But Mum Williams was unfazed.

"It's not goin' to 'appen. Not in Croydon! Them Beatles fans are all screaming so loud any missile pointin' at England will turn round and fly the uvver way in fright!"

****

By the terribly cold winter of 1962/63 I was becoming more adept at avoiding my father's attentions, possibly because I was able to go out when I felt the threatening signs, or it could have been because by that stage he had turned his lascivious eyes towards my youngest sibling. Whatever the cause, I still felt uncomfortable and as if I did not completely belong, whenever I was chatting with my old school friends and young colleagues from work.

I had lost my innocence. When my colleagues and friends were giggling about things they had tried with boys, or more risqué things that they were fantasising about trying, I sat with them, pretending to take part in the conversation, whilst thinking how misguided they were and how one day they would find out the truth.

Occasionally, when we were all playing Happy Families at the weekend, the five of us would pile into my father's car and we would drive down to visit Uncle Noel and Auntie Peggy. I still adored my aunt and uncle and I was fascinated by the rest of my father's extended family, most of whom I had never met. I had another aunt called Molly who had 16 children, so she was rather busy, but her eldest son, Tom, had paid us a visit when he returned from a tour of duty in Aden.

Although Flora was cold as a fridge to her daughters, she fussed around Tom like a mother hen. He was attractive in a typically Irish way with almost black hair and beautiful eyes. When he visited Hedley Drive it was summer time and he was tanned from the Arab sun. Although we reckoned it was a balmy day, he was wrapped up in a padded Air Force bomber jacket and immediately asked my mother to switch on the gas fire. She danced around him in her girlish, flirty way, plying him with food and lapping up his attention every time he called her Auntie Flo. Both my parents called him "Good old Tom", in contrast to the way they would ridicule and imitate some of the other nephews and nieces if they had strong Irish accents or seemed weedy in any way.

Although Flora could do small spiteful things to Peggy due to her jealousy, she remained besotted by my uncle and always refused to leave my father in a room with Noel for fear that he might "show me up". This allowed me to develop a good relationship with my aunt and she would teach me many of the domestic skills she had learnt whilst she was in service which, as it didn't involve cooking or needlework, I loved.

One day when I was helping my aunt to clear away lunch I told her that my father did things to me. I think I wanted to gain her sympathy and get her to say something critical of her brother. Nobody in the family ever said a word against "Gerry" for leaving his children to be cared for by other people, or for any other reason. We had been brought up in the Protestant faith and my mother was a Protestant, yet all my father's family were staunch Catholics. I felt that the different religions often made an unbridgeable distance between us. I wanted to cross over to their side, for my aunt to fight for me and look shocked at her niece's plight.

She let out a little laugh.

"Get over it Kiddo, in Ireland that's normal family life!"

****

I finally plucked up the courage to go to the Croydon Operatic and Dramatic Association (CODA) for an audition. I took my sheet music with me and the lady at the piano was very encouraging and congratulated me on singing beautifully. However, it was a dramatic association so it required me to move as well as sing. I was sent along to see the choreographer. I sat with some other hopefuls and then she called me out on stage. She looked at my cuboid form standing there for what seemed like an eternity before saying in a shrill, sarcastic voice,

"… ***can*** you move?"

Although they offered me a place I couldn't get out of the door quick enough. I never went back.

My mother was always full of advice about my weight. She was somehow convinced that eating certain foods actually caused you to lose weight. Over the years there were a number of different substances that fell into the category of being, "Very slimming you know Margaret. You ought to buy it. You'll be slim in no time."

If you gave my mother a penny for her thoughts, you'd probably get change!

****

It was the summer of the Profumo scandal and the Great Train Robbery. Obviously the Profumo affair was deeply shocking and could only be discussed at 21A behind a primly placed Victorian hand, with a voice dropped so low you would have thought we were bugged by MI5.

There was a sliding reaction to the train robbers. At first there was a sense that they were folk heroes, akin to Robin Hood and his merry men who had managed to get away with 2.6 million pounds in untraceable bank notes due to brilliant planning. To begin with the feeling in our household was "good luck to 'em", but once it came out that a guard had been coshed the gang morphed into highway men.

Violence wasn't acceptable whatever the prize.

****

"I'm staying at home tonight," I said to Flora as I left for work on Friday morning. She knew that meant I would be at 21A, I had never left them in any doubt about where "home" was.

Ever since the days when we were very young and anyone at the Friday evening gathering might have been asked to put their hands in their pockets for new shoes, neither of my parents had ever shown their face at 21A on a Friday afternoon. If my father was picking us up, we would wait until we saw his car and then go out to him, there was never any Friday interaction. So I always felt safe and fully relaxed at 21A on Fridays, able to bask in their happiness at the groceries I had brought.

This particular Friday Mum Williams had just unpacked all of my goodies onto the kitchen table. Christine had walked back from school with Tina and they were in the kitchen with the rest of us. The two of them would usually have to wait another couple of hours before my father drove round the corner to take them back to Hedley Drive for the weekend. Suddenly Christine looked through the window and shouted, "Mum's outside!"

Mum Williams tried scooping the goods off the table and hobbling towards the scullery whilst hissing at Hilda, "Quick! Open the front door and get 'er in the front room, don't let 'er see this!"

Hilda leapt to her post and persuaded Flora that the back door was stuck so she had to come into the front room. We so nearly got away with it, but Christine was too young to realise what was going on and said, "look at all the lovely groceries Margy's bought this week! She always brings lovely things on Fridays."

Flora's face set like thunder, "Is that so?" she said settling herself into Hilda's chair to be waited on by Mum Williams.

When I got home the following day, my mother was waiting for me, "'ow much do you spend on them?"

"I don't spend much, under a pound, maybe 18 shillings."

"Right then, I'll have an extra pound off you every week from now on."

I had no option but to tell Mum Williams, "Don't worry about that, tell 'er to stick 'er pound!" she said.

"I'll still buy you things Mum …"
"I've told you not to, I've always told you not to …"
"I will anyway, somehow …"

Chapter thirteen

I was due to have another eye operation. I had known it was pending for some time which was why I hadn't applied for any clerical jobs. I stared at myself in my bedroom mirror. Although my eyes were still not pointing in the same direction I recognised that they were my father's eyes and that this part of me looked like him. It was a shock. With our white blonde hair, Tina and I both most obviously resembled my mother, but as I looked at my eyes I was forced to admit to myself that in many ways I was more like him than her.

Gerard was an amusing character, quick witted and intent on making everyone laugh. He included the whole world in his *joie de vivre*, his daughters too. In all the photographs I saw of him, he was surrounded by people, the life and soul of any party. Gerry, everybody's friend, who could talk himself up to be the big man even if he didn't have a penny in his pocket. My father was all about show, which would explain why he told the council we were at boarding school! He had to keep up the act that he was a man of substance. By contrast, Uncle Noel actually was, but he never blew his own trumpet, people found out about Noel's achievements slowly.

I knew there wouldn't be any hospital visits with grapes or flowers from my parents when I went in for my next eye operation. There never were.

Strangely, ever since Christine and I moved to her house, my mother had developed memories of motherhood, which were quite bizarre given her complete lack of normal maternal care. When talking to neighbours, or even just to us, Flora would suddenly spout out stories about things we used to do when we were toddlers. If there were other people around, Christine and I would look at each other and raise our eyebrows, but if we were in her house I no longer tiptoed around my mother's feelings.

"How do you know? You were never there!"

"Honestly Margaret, I can't understand why you are so angry and horrible the whole time when we've given you so much ..." Then she would descend into one of her sulks until my father nuzzled her neck and talked to her like a child to bring her out of it again. I wanted to ask her "why didn't you love us like a normal mother," but part of me knew I would never get the answer I wanted, so I used contempt instead.

With my father my feelings were more complicated. Although I loathed him for what he had done, I wanted a proper Dad – far more than I wanted a proper Mum. Proper Dads protect you. I didn't know how to unlock those loving paternal feelings and have them directed towards me. It was an aspect of him that I imagine Christine experienced. I would have sold my soul for a Dad like that.

****

It was a cold day in late November and directly I got out of hospital I headed to 21A in my NHS eye patch, ready for a dose of TLC from Mum Williams. The Rolling Stones had recently hit the big time and Cyril was recounting his story about "knowin' dem Stones…" yet again to Tina as they stood in the yard at the front of the house. Cyril was heading for the old shop door to tend to the baby crocodile he was keeping there in a cage. I had no idea where he got the reptile from and I wasn't about to give him the satisfaction of asking him. He may have been a man and so able to force some liberties in the house, but he still wasn't allowed in the front room or invited to any family meals. Whatever else he got away with, he would never be welcomed.

"Where's Mum?" I asked my sister. She tossed her head towards the kitchen before announcing she was on an errand to go and buy some broken biscuits for Mum to dunk in her tea. "Don't worry, I've brought custard tarts, there's one here for you too if you want it."

I was back in the heart of my family, sitting on the old brown sofa next to Mum after our tea. Then the day stopped. The pictures from America started playing over and over again. Pictures of a huge black open top car. Pictures of a woman in a pale dress throwing herself across her husband. Pictures of the assassination of a young, dynamic man. It was totally shocking. The black and white news reel matched the dark evening outside our windows. There were no other items, just the same pictures round and round in a loop until they formally announced President Kennedy was dead. Everything was paralysed except for Mum rocking beside me breathing, "Oo my gawd! Oo my gawd! Nooo!"

****

I don't know if it was because I had been removed from my family at 21A, but I felt displaced. My mother's house wasn't my "home". This was made clear in so many ways, not just the nightly striptease, the open loo door, the lack of affection and the abuse, but little things like when a postcard arrived and I asked who it was from, she replied, "Give that to me, it's from one of *our* friends." I wasn't a part of my parents' lives. Now that I didn't live at 21A I didn't feel as much a part of their lives either. Although I visited often, nobody was waiting for me to arrive home any more. There was nobody I really belonged to, so I went in search of my father's family in the hope that they would enfold me with widely flung arms as long lost kin.

First I went to visit Aunt Molly and my 16 cousins. I had planned my trip meticulously, wanting to make the best impression on my blood relatives. The experience didn't exactly live up to my expectations; it was similar to visiting the old woman who lived in the shoe! Although Aunt Molly had 16 children, the eldest eight of them had begun to produce children of their own so that aunts and uncles were younger than nieces and nephews. Aunt Molly was so hard pressed to feed all the mouths that she used one of the huge zinc containers Mum Williams employed to wash nappies in, to cook her "pataties" and then dumped the whole thing in the middle of the table for everyone to help themselves out of it. Her husband, Uncle Mike, rolled through the door at the end of the "meal" blind drunk, and crashed into bed with his cement-covered boots still on his feet. Eventually I excused myself and headed for the train station. While I was enthralled with them, they obviously weren't the slightest bit interested in me. There was too much already going on in their family to absorb anyone from "outside".

Next I tried to integrate myself with a cousin more my own age. Kitty was one of Aunt Molly's eldest daughters. She had had a twin who had died, so I rather hoped she might be looking for a new sister figure. My own sisters were so much younger than me that there was no possibility of sharing any of my teenage angst with them or talking to them about what was on Radio Luxembourg or Radio Caroline on a Saturday night. At that age they could never provide the sort of relationship I was searching for, they were still little children.

Kitty was married to a boy who was mean to her and regularly left her in the house with no money to feed their two children. I turned up on a Sunday morning, which I thought would be a good time, but my choice just served to highlight the deep differences between Protestants and Catholics. I arrived as they were about to go to church. There was no way they would miss Mass, so they just left me in the house on my own. Kitty didn't need any more family, religious observance was far more important.

Gerard would always be welcomed in his sister's houses, but we Protestants were a different breed. We were something to be slightly suspicious of; an inconvenient family hiccup.

Peggy and Noel remained the only real family I could be close to and, out of the two of them, it was Noel – the one who was not my blood relative – who was my favourite.

One weekend when we were down at Peggy and Noel's, my father's cousin was over from Ireland plus a few other grown up relatives, so we children had to be quiet – seen but not heard. After a while Noel beckoned us into the television room.

"Shall we go and look at the waves?"

There was a little bay at Seaford where it was always rough. We played at walking under the waves before they crashed down on the beach and came back completely soaked – and completely elated! The four of us crept into the house by the back door, nipped swiftly up the stairs, then Noel put us all into different bedrooms with a couple of towels each so we could make ourselves as presentable as possible before we re-entered the adult fray and received the disapproving stares that were guaranteed. However, as it was Noel who had led us astray, we were certain Flora wouldn't go completely bonkers because to do so would "show 'er up"!

On my sixteenth birthday Uncle Noel arrived at Hedley Drive with an immense baker's tray of Rum Babas for my party – although it was technically "my party" I don't think there were many of my friends there, it was mainly Gerard's family and work contacts plus Patsy from next door. There were certainly more Rum Babas than people, but Uncle Noel always did things to make you feel special, there was no way he would just bring a bag of five or six, he wanted to show me that turning sixteen was a big deal, and I loved him for it.

****

Whenever I left home on a Friday morning the last words Flora would say to me were, "don't forget to leave my money on the kitchen table as soon as you get in".

Despite the fact that she was taking most of my earnings, I was good at managing my money and was still able to buy a few groceries for Mum Williams and save a little every week towards a motorbike. I dreamed of a Lambretta - such style - I could picture myself on a scarlet one looking super chic as I sped along, but to be honest, any wheels would do and I was already counting the days to my seventeenth birthday when I could take my driving test.

Although I could no longer afford to take princely quantities of exotic foods to Mum Williams, I would always try to take a Fray Bentos pie for Kath and a few other bits and pieces. Kath adored those pies. The tin came with a little key which allowed you to roll back the lid and then put the whole thing in the oven so that the pastry rose out of the open tin to give a crisp brown topping.

Unfortunately Kath wasn't the most delicate person on earth and could be quite heavy handed. One day she went to open the pie and the key broke off so that she couldn't roll back the top. She tried to use a normal tin opener, but there was no lip on the tin so it was impossible to attach it. Then she stabbed it with a knife to try and cut round it, but only made a series of dents. By this time the rest of the family had gathered round and were making variety of unhelpful suggestions as Kath became very red in the face. She was absolutely determined to have her pie, more so than ever because both Marjory and Hilda were laughing at her frustration.

"Gimme a tea towel Mum," she growled before stomping out to the yard.

"Whatcha doin'?" Mum was yelling as Kath delved about in the back of the car. Tight lipped and grim faced she placed the tea towel over the tin and started working on it with a hammer and chisel.

"Give it 'ere. I'll get it out for you," Charlie piped up as the chisel just added to the dents the knife had already made.

Everyone ended up having a go, but those tins were completely bomb proof without the flimsy little key. The whole incident was unforgettable because it was the only time I ever saw food being thrown in the dustbin at Nell's house. The Fray Bentos pie had triumphed where every other edible scrap had failed!

****

The house at 21A was still as manic as ever and it was grubby too now that Cyril had swapped his crocodile for a dog because the croc had eaten all the putty out of the sides of its cage and escaped into the shop. The croc had been growing rapidly. It definitely had to go, but I have no idea how Cyril eventually disposed of it.

Although the dog made the house smelly, 21A was never spick and span. Everything in it was very, very old. The lino was wearing away in many places. Mum, Kath and Hilda weren't the type of people to buy new furniture - they made-do and mended. This grimy crumbling house was still more of a home in my eyes than my mother's modern pristine box where there were never any photos of us children on display. Mum Williams' Best Room, at the top of the stairs, where her marital bedroom had been, remained stuffed with displays of our achievements at school, photographs of all of us were framed and hung from the picture rail, plus a host of cared-for old toys were kept in boxes so that they could be used for all the new babies who still turned up in prams when hard pushed local mothers needed a helping hand.

****

I was very aware that my weekend disappearances to Mum Williams' house irritated my father greatly. It seemed as if every time I left the house he responded with more anger and a growing certainty that I was destined to descend into an abyss of slutty behaviour if I wasn't kept closely guarded at Hedley Drive. However I stuck to the story that I was going to "stay at home" in front of him even if I was intending to sleep at a friend's house.

Every time I dodged being alone with my father he became furious, drumming his fingers on the chair arms and grinding his teeth. If I said I was going out with friends or to a dance the accusations would come thick and fast. His imagination of my social life was exceedingly colourful and the spiral of crude allegations would expand every time he pictured me enjoying myself.

Ivy's husband, Cliff, finally provided me with a method of escape that meant I didn't even have to wait for a bus before fleeing. The Lambretta I coveted was way out of my price range, but Cliff found me an NSU which he paid twelve pounds for and allowed me to pay off in instalments. I was literally bursting with excitement when I saw it parked in the yard at 21A. Naturally, Mum Williams was full of all the warnings about accidents, speed, wet roads, lorries and anything else she could think of, but I was in heaven. I had wheels. I had freedom.

Friday and Saturday nights became the time to go to Wardour Street which was where all the early groups played. I saw The Who, The Troggs and The Yardbirds there, all before they became famous. Unfortunately The Beatles never played there, but my group of friends were all Beatles fans. We danced a lot, we had a lot of parties, but we didn't get drunk, we didn't have the money or the inclination. The weekends were for fun, and being hung over wouldn't be fun, so we didn't do it.

As I was now only a temporary lodger at 21A and nobody knew if I would be there or not, I enjoyed more freedom than many teenagers. One night I walked up the road with Mary Nightingale at about 11 o'clock to find Nell propping herself up against the gate anxiously looking up and down the street.

"Oh Mum, I'm so sorry, am I late?"

"No you're not, but when I see that Kath she's going to get a piece of my mind!"

Kath would have been in her forties by then, but as far as her mother was concerned it wasn't proper for her to be out at night, and no "scandalous" behaviour would ever be attached to her girls as long as she was still in the driving seat, however old they might be. At 16 I had the liberty to do as I chose, but the spinsters of 21A did not!

Chapter 14

With the latest operation completed, both of my eyes were pointing roughly in the same direction and I felt more confident to apply for career posts, rather than just jobs. Also I wanted to stop having to work on Saturdays. I soon left the toy shop and got a job at Longbank, which then became Longbard and eventually Nat West.

I started in the Central Filing Department, which was where all the girls started unless they were highly skilled. In Filing you had to prove your aptitudes in different ways before you could apply for promotion. The department itself was enormous with thousands of paper files. Every girl was timed in and out of the department, even when we went to the Ladies.

Gladys was in charge of us. She always twiddled her hair and always had a cigarette hanging from her mouth. For me she was a mimic's dream, so I used to make people laugh quite a lot. When it was quiet the girls used to say, "Come on, do your Gladys!", but often I would find she was standing behind me without my noticing. She was all right about it however. We liked Gladys; she always gave a Christmas party for all the filing girls which was quite an energetic affair.

"Most people end up dropping, and there are just loads of bodies on the floor in the morning," one of the senior girls told me.

"Just make sure you don't have the breakfast if you wake up hungry," Jean Webb added before the big event.

"Is she a really terrible cook?" I asked.

"No, it's nothing to do with the cooking, but there's always a load of cigarette ash in the bacon and eggs!"

Longbank was completely different to any of the jobs I had been in before. There was a whole crowd of young people and we were invited to dinner dances by the men from the post office and other large firms in the area. I suddenly had a whole social network from the office and some of the girls became long term friends. There was Jean Webb, but also Valerie Brigdedon and Cynthia Hodely who was a tall girl, a bit like Janet Street Porter to look at - she works in television now. Once we progressed from filing, our wages became really good. Suddenly I was getting five pounds a week, and although Flora was ensuring she still received the lion's share, I was able to start buying Friday night groceries for Mum Williams again without a problem.

Jean Webb was becoming my special friend at Longbank. We had the same afternoon off during the week and often went to dances together at the weekends. Jean had lots of reddish brown hair and a pretty face all of which drew attention away from what she considered to be her awful flaw – a pair of rather big ankles.

We used to get Luncheon Vouchers at work, but we could have a packed lunch on Fridays if we wished. Most of the girls in filing would opt for the packed lunch so that we could go shopping and one of us would be designated to dash down and pick up all the lunches whilst the others started out for the centre of town. There were a number of shops that stocked extremely cheap clothes, all perfect for parties, but so poorly made that if we bought them on Friday and wore them on Saturday they generally were in the bin by Sunday.

Jean was at a loose end on one of our afternoons off and asked to tag along with me as I announced I was going shopping and then heading down to see Mum Williams. I had told Mum all about Jean so I knew she would be delighted to meet her. We arrived with the usual bag of custard tarts but Mum was instantly thinking about feeding us.

"You see!" I said turning to Jean, "Same old Mum, you won't get away without a meal!"

"Please don't go to any trouble Mrs Williams," Jean said, "Just some toast would be lovely."

"I've got some beans …"

"That would be great Mum, beans on toast."

But, as usual, the table cloth had to come out, the places laid, the tomato sauce, brown sauce and all the other bits and pieces brought painstakingly out of the kitchen on her wobbly legs, one by one, as she refused to let us help, insisting that we "take the weight off yer legs, you'll be dancing half the night if I know you youngsters …" A plate of bread and butter emerged and then two plates each with two rounds of toast and an entire can of beans on each of them, by this time Jean's jaw was practically on the floor.

"My goodness Mrs Williams, this is a banquet!" Jean said, sounding rather worried and as if she might not be able to manage the vast portion.

"Go on, eat it all up, I've done it all nice for you."

By the time we left we could hardly move. "I'm staying at Jean's flat tonight Mum because it's closer to the dance, but I'll see you tomorrow," I said as she set her last custard tart aside to have later.

"Thank you for the meal Mrs Williams, it was so nice to meet you."

Once we got round the corner Jean hugged her stomach, "Oh my goodness Maggie there's no way I'll be able to jive tonight, if any boy tries to lift me up he'll break his back!"

But when it came to it, we still danced for all we were worth. From the moment we had put our handbags into the coat check we were on the floor. It was free to go in and dance but drinks were expensive so we could make one bitter lemon last all night. Obviously if any lad asked us what we were drinking we said "Gin and bitter lemon", but we would be doing really well if we managed to get more than one or two drinks, maximum, bought for us during the whole evening.

By the time we left our feet ached so much it was more comfortable to walk home barefoot, so we did, arriving at the flat with our high heels in our hands and our soles completely black. Jean's mum was lovely and made us hot chocolate whilst we soaked our sore feet in bowls of warm soapy water and told her all the evening's events before dropping into bed and sleeping until noon.

****

It was late January and Winston Churchill had finally died of a stroke. Although he wasn't a member of the royal family it was felt that he was such an icon of Britain that he merited a state funeral with a gun carriage, the royal family fully represented in black and a day off work for the entire nation. The death had been expected for some time and Operation Hope Not swung into force with smooth efficiency immediately to ensure the country had a funeral to remember.

I stayed at 21A the night before the funeral and woke to find the house already prepared for a TV marathon. The sofa and Hilda's chair were in optimum position to see the black and white screen and the curtains were pulled tight shut to keep out the daylight. Winston Churchill had been lying in state at Westminster Hall for several days and despite the freezing cold weather the queues of mourners had stretched for over a mile and the Hall was kept open 23 hours a day.

By 9.30 all the family, apart from my parents, were ranged in front of the telly. Tea cups were at the ready together with bits of handiwork. I fished an envelope full of Green Shield stamps out of my bag and handed them over to Nell, "I keep forgetting to give you these."

"That'll keep me busy," Mum said, heaving herself off the sofa to retrieve the book that was already half full of the small green stamps. "That tight bugger down at the petrol station only gave Kath 10 the other day, I told 'er to go somewhere else if 'e's as stingy again!"

Everyone collected Green Shield Stamps. They were given away at shops, petrol stations and practically anywhere else you paid for anything, but how many you received for the amount spent used to be exceedingly flexible. Although it took several books full to obtain anything more interesting than a nailbrush in return, the nation was hooked on the new idea of something for nothing. Green Shield Stamps was like a little bit of Christmas every day! Needless to say, Nell was addicted to collecting them.

By the time Big Ben struck for the final time that day, at 9.45, Nell was busily wiping her tongue over each of the stamps and proudly sticking them in the book, albeit somewhat wonkily because she kept looking up at the TV and being transfixed by the pomp and ceremony of it all. There was a magnificent military procession from the Palace of Westminster to St Pauls, the route's pavement crammed with crowds whose expressions oscillated between pride and grief. The velvet voice of Richard Dimbleby guided the nation through the service as our hearts swelled to the sound of "I vow to thee my country".

I was glad for the dimness of our front room when Elgar's Nimrod began to be played. As it burgeoned into its full sad majesty the hairs on the back of my neck rose and an involuntary tear slid down my face as I heard, for the first time, what I still consider to be one of the world's most beautiful piece of music.

As the trumpeter sounded the Last Post, the coffin headed off to Tower Pier and a 19-gun salute. Mum Williams was instantly back on her feet bringing out tea and scones.

"The old guard are goin' now," she said as she put out the jam, "It shudda been me, I've 'ad my time …" A good funeral always made Mum a little morbid. In fact we had to make soothing noises to the same words every time the obituaries were read out of the Croydon paper, but like many people in Britain, the funeral of her wartime hero had touched her deeply. The upside with Nell was that if she could get an extra slice of victoria sponge down someone, her troubles were instantly forgotten and life was good again, so we ensured she was never morose for long.

****

It was far more difficult to cheer up Flora. She didn't need a funeral to make her unhappy, in fact that came far down her list of bad occurrences. Envy and not being complimented on her appearance were much closer to the top. Gerard spent much of his life attempting to mitigate these situations, yet Flora still spent a considerable part of her life sulking.

Around this time Peggy and Noel were coming to a big Masonic evening in our area. Rather than drive all the way in their finery and arrive rather crushed, Peggy assumed they would be welcome to change at my parents' house. It may have been that my father had told her there would be no problem as, obviously, there shouldn't have been. Peggy and Noel were the last people on earth Gerard would have wanted to upset, but my mother was so jealous of Peggy's social life, and her wardrobe full of cocktail dresses, that she flatly refused to allow her through the front door. Without giving any reason, Flora rang Peggy and told her she could not come.

This time envy triumphed over being "shown up" in front of Noel. Although my Aunt and Uncle were upset at the time, they weren't the type to brood on Flora's peak. It certainly took far longer for my mother to stop sulking than for them to get back on a normal footing with Gerard and me.

****

Although I saw far less of Mary Nightingale since we went to separate schools, we still kept in touch and that summer, shortly after the Train Robber Ronnie Biggs escaped over the wall of Wandsworth Prison, we headed off on my NSU to spend three nights at a campsite in Devil's Dike in Brighton. The "Ton-up boys" – Mods and Rockers hell bent on trying to reach 100 miles per hour on their Vespas and Lambrettas - had caused some trouble on Brighton beach the year before but we didn't see why that should bother us.

We were having a great time, a couple of other friends had also turned up at the campsite and we had met a group of Dutch boys whose English was surprisingly good. Half way through our stay the campsite owner came round and told everybody they had to pack up and leave immediately because the local police had heard there was going to be big trouble between the Mods and the Rockers. The police were insisting that any innocent bystanders be moved out of the way as quickly as possible.

As we didn't want to abandon our holiday and Uncle Noel lived along the road in Peacehaven, I headed off to the phone box.

Peggy and Noel were cool, especially with young people, they didn't miss a beat before offering beds to me and my three friends. They also allowed the unknown Dutch boys to camp on their lawn as they hadn't got a ferry home for some days and certainly didn't have the money for a hotel.

There was no hesitation, "OK Kiddo, bring them all along!"

Everyone needs an uncle or aunt like that!

Soon after our Brighton jaunt I sold my NSU as my seventeenth birthday was looming and I was desperate to drive … instantly!

I passed my test after just nine lessons and, strangely enough, my father bought me my first car for 15 guineas. It was an A30, a tiny bubbly thing that you could have in any colour so long as it was grey or black. Mine was grey.

We had to pick it up from the bottom of Caterham Hill, but the car didn't make it to the top of the hill so the garage had to come out and tow it back to Croydon while somebody Gerard knew came and sorted it out. I was desperate to get behind the wheel of my own car, so I was praying that nothing major was wrong.

Directly it was mended I decided to have a cruise around Croydon High Street and buy my first tank of petrol. There was a little pull in garage where they used to wipe your windscreen with a leather and check your oil as part of the service. The man came out to me with a polite, "Yes, Miss..."

"I need a gallon of petrol please." So he gave me that and wiped my windscreen.

"Check your oil, Miss?"

"Yes, please," I said feeling so proud and wheel-happy.

"It's a bit low, Miss."

"I'll have a gallon of oil too then!"

Perhaps I didn't know very much about what was beneath my car bonnet, but I was still the speed queen of Croydon! I loved putting my foot down and I can park on a sixpence. At this time only 13 per cent of women had driving licenses while 56 per cent of men drove. Women were meant to be passengers, but I put myself firmly in the driving seat. If Kath could do it, so would I.

Not that I always drove, certainly not when I went out for an evening with Jean. She knew a different set of people in Croydon to the ones I had gone to school with and there were always dances in her part of town. One night we were at the Orchard Ballroom in Purley, walking behind a small stage to reach the dance floor when a boy shouted out, "Hello Jean". She turned and smiled broadly at the lad, "Hello John".

John was with a friend who had a big grin etched on his face. We carried on to the dance floor, stoically refusing to look backwards while desperately hoping they were watching us. We began to dance. Suddenly John grabbed hold of Jean and a friendly voice said, "Would you like to dance, I'm Ken."

Chapter 15

Apologies for the double negative, but it was impossible not to like Ken! He was very personable and very intelligent but I immediately discovered that he could not dance. This was unfortunate because he knew everything about current music and couldn't get enough of it, but rhythm never got as far as his feet. To give him his due, he never stopped trying! When we collapsed onto chairs for a brief respite from the dance floor, I discovered he also shared my love of classical music. I love Puccini, Mendelsohn, Chopin, Schubert and Brook and I also love jazz. Ken was a jazz enthusiast but his classical tastes were a little more austere than mine and included Wagner, Rimsky-Korsakov and much of the dramatic music from the major ballets.

He, like me, was very involved with his local church and I quickly suspected his family life was odd, although to begin with I couldn't put my finger on why.

At this stage in my life I sounded like a conventional 18 year old. I lived with my parents and had a job in a bank. Ken, while being very complimentary about his parents, had supported himself in a small bedsit since he was 15 and was doing five years of printing indentures.

His smile was infectious, even if he couldn't jive like Phillip. As we flung ourselves round the dance floor in uncoordinated heaven, we agreed on how great it was that The Beatles were to be given MBEs and how daft all the old codgers were who were returning their war medals to Her Majesty in protest at the Fab Four's honour.

"Do you think they'll find a way of stopping it?" I asked.

"Nah, they'll have to go through with it now, anyway Harold Wilson must have wanted it. The stiffs will just have to get used to it!"

It seems incredible today that anyone would think that Paul McCartney and the rest of them were corrupting the morals of Britain, but at the time the newspapers were filled with indignant letters and articles that seemed to predict England would become a sleazy den of corruption if any sort of official recognition were given to something as innocuous as "Love, love me do"! We relished it. My generation finally seemed to be edging out from beneath the thumb of Victorian prudishness.

John and Jean stayed together all evening so Ken and I did the same. As we separated to return to Jean's house Ken said, "How about you come with me to my church group tomorrow?"

"I could do … if you'll come to mine next week."

"Deal," he said with his great grin and a friendly wave as he headed off with John, "See you tomorrow."

****

Ken's church group was much the same as mine, a bunch of pleasant young people who enjoyed being active parts of their communities. Afterwards he began to walk me back to Mum Williams' house, "You must come in for a cup of tea, my Nan would love to meet you, I'm sure you'd hit it off."

"Maybe I could come round sometime next week," Ken sounded a little hesitant. "I have to go and visit my father now, he's not well and things get difficult if there are changes or I'm not around when he expects me."

"What's wrong with him?"

"He's got schizophrenia, it's very hard on Mum. He set fire to the house in the middle of the night recently. He's been a bit calmer since I moved out but he still has bad episodes. When I lived there we used to wash and then get into our clothes again to go to bed because of the number of times we'd have to get up and go down the street with him to mend the car in the middle of the night, or something equally strange! He gets nervous if Mum and I are together and he's not in the room … thinks we're plotting against him. It's hard for him, but on Sunday afternoons my grandmother visits and he'll often come into the front room for an hour and talk to all of us."

"Can the doctors help him?"

"He has lots of different medications but some of them make him very sleepy and he can be asleep for three days at a stretch. Mum has to try to watch him as sometimes he won't take them, or else he'll take half a bottle!"

A bright red Morris Minor adorned with yellow and green flowers drove past us and stopped a little further up the street. A couple of women in long colourful dresses stepped out. One of them started to go into a terraced house, a heavy peace-symbol necklace jumping in front of her as she walked, we could see her grubby feet in Indian leather flip-flops beneath the grimy hem of her skirt. Her friend bent down to speak through the passenger window, long hair swinging down so that one of the many flowers in it fell onto the pavement.

Ken looked at me and raised an eyebrow, "Fancy an Afghan coat for Christmas?" he said with a grin.

"They must be on something!" I said. "Did you see her toenails? Ugg!"

When people think back to the 60s there's a feeling that all young people were discovering sex and drugs and rock 'n' roll. Most of us were excited about the more liberal music but, as for the drugs and sex scene, the majority of people were living normal lives in normal jobs – although as it wasn't the likes of us who made the front pages of the newspapers, that tends to be forgotten. There was once a whisper about some drugs being used around the ice rink in Croydon and we were told to be careful, but other than that it didn't touch us in the slightest.

I had left my car at 21A so that I could stay as long as possible before driving home for the start of the new working week. My father would be dropping Tina back at Mum Williams' in a couple of hours after her weekend at Hedley Drive, but I could stay longer and have tea with the family. Tina was 11 and would soon begin secondary school where Christine had already started. Before Ken left me I had to quickly show him my car.

"What car do you want to buy?" I asked, anticipating that he, like me, was thinking of cars, wheels and speed for much of the day.

"I've never thought about it," he said, looking a little puzzled.

"...but you can drive?"

"No, I've never touched a steering wheel."

My mouth dropped open, I had thought we had everything in common, this needed rectifying. "Looks like I'll need to teach you!"

"I'll keep you to that," he said with a smile as he walked towards the bus stop for his afternoon vigil at his father's house.

****

It was a relief that 21A was as noisy as usual. It would allow me to quietly think about my weekend without interruption.

Hilda was attempting to boil a kettle of water so that she could replenish the tea and tiptoe back down to Cyril in the basement, but Kath was taking great pleasure in baiting her while the cries of "Stop 'er Mum, I ain't done nuffin' to 'er!" just egged Kath on to greater inventiveness in her insults. Mum Williams slapped the newspaper down on the kitchen table, "now stop it, the two of you, I'm tryin' t'read the paper!"

"Hello Mum," I said from the back door.

"Hello Margy, you 'ad a good day? I'll get you a cup of tea."

"No need Mum, Hilda's already got the kettle going, can I get you anything?"

"No fanks luv, 'ere looks like they's definitely goin' to get rid of the death penalty," she said stabbing an arthritic finger at a column of the paper. "Not that it will do Mrs Bentley any good, poor soul."

"Nor them kiddies of Ruth Ellis," Kath added

"Ooo my lawd, there's been too many mistakes! Remember that Timothy Evans, dreadful, simply dreadful ..." while Hilda slipped out of the kitchen door with her teapot and the rest of us settled down to chime in with nods and grunts to any other gems of information that Nell found in the local rag.

****

Employment at the printing presses meant that Ken often worked long late shifts, but we still managed to grab odd times together at record shops or the cinema. We could spend hours at the record shops attached to the big headphones they provided in the booths, listening to the latest sounds and deciding whether we liked them enough to put our hand in our pockets. The major film out was *The Sound of Music*, about seven children who went through a rather wobbly time but then got a new mother and everything was wonderful. As it was based on truth it made me a little nostalgic. The same thing didn't seem to happen in Croydon!

As I had expected, Mum Williams and Kath got on brilliantly with Ken, although Kath was as insistent as I was that he should waste no more time before he learnt how to drive. Nell was in heaven as she had found a new man to cook and make cups of tea for. There was no hesitation in letting Ken join the family in the front room, although Cyril remained taboo.

****

On the second Sunday after we met, Ken asked if I would accompany him on his weekly visit to his parents' house. He had already met Mum Williams and the rest of the clan at 21A and come to my church group, so it seemed churlish not to accept although I was pretty apprehensive.

A small, thin, nervous woman opened the front door. She wasn't a nice looking lady. Her nose appeared to carry on past her mouth which was very wide and thin. Her legs were skinny and bowed, a strange mottling of the skin was clearly visible through her stockings and her head was surrounded by a mass of dark curly hair.

"Hello Mum, I'd like you to meet Maggie," the smile that had been on her wide, thin mouth when she saw her son, set. She turned her face to me and put out a hand, "Pleased to meet you." We shook and she let us in to the narrow dingy hallway.

"I'm just making the tea, perhaps you could help me Ken, I've got a couple of things in the kitchen for you. Would you like to sit in here?" she said to me, opening a side door onto the front room.

A very old woman was perched on the edge of one of the chairs. She was short and as round as she was tall. I was forced to inch past her to get to a chair so I smiled nervously and squeaked out a "Good afternoon." Her only reply was to click her dentures in and out whilst looking at me like an angry English bulldog. As we shared the silence I noticed how decrepit the house was.

It was dirty and there were electrical wires hanging from the walls and disappearing through doorways, the skirting board finished with an inch gap before the start of the floorboards, and I tried not to think about what might inhabit the space between the two. Eventually Ken and his mother, Lillian, arrived with the tea and cake. Ken had a string bag hanging from his wrist with a packet of biscuits, a loaf of bread and a jar of jam in it, "Extra rations from Mum," he said with a smile as he sat down next to me and passed tea to his grandmother.

Lillian was pouring tea quickly, "Can I leave you to cut the cake Maggie, Denis has just called for me," and she dashed off into the bedroom with two cups of tea.

"He gets nervous when we are all out here together," Ken explained. "He has different buttons he can press for the intercoms in different rooms, that's why there are all these wires around the walls. We'll probably get called in next."

"I don't have to come in if it might upset him."

"I think he'll like to meet you," Ken replied. "We'll see how it goes."

The denture clicking continued while we ate our cake and drank tea. It seemed to drown out the possibility of any conversation.

"Excuse me, could you show me where the loo is?" I whispered to Ken.

"The loo?" Clearly there was nothing wrong with her hearing!

The old woman's tone was dripping with contempt, "We never spoke of such things in my day. In all my years of marriage I never once told my husband I was going to the water closet, yet you've known my grandson five minutes!" she tossed her head and went back to clicking her teeth whilst my face burned with embarrassment as Ken propelled me outside.

"Don't take any notice, she's just a bit Victorian and she's probably worried he won't call for her. She only comes on Sundays."

I couldn't help thinking about Mum Williams and how she made everyone, even Paper Jack, feel as welcome as possible, yet this old lady who had some fancy house in East Croydon was hell bent on making me feel like a worm before I'd had a chance to show her I wasn't a bad person. I sat for as long as possible, hoping that she might have gone in to see her son by the time I got back, but fate wasn't on my side and I had to run the gauntlet of her withering stare before making it safely to my seat beside Ken.

She sat there clicking until Ken's Mum came in and said we should go and see his father. My desire to get away from Ken's grandmother, who was now looking at me as though burning at the stake would be too good for me, was only just stronger than my fear of what I was about to encounter in the bedroom.

Ken opened the door onto a stale stench. Inside the room it smelt as if a variety of small animals had died. Sitting up in bed was a withered man with mad-professor hair and darting sunken eyes. Ken introduced me, but I remained close to the door in case my presence upset his Dad. Ken sat beside the bed and I could hear him describe his week but the replies from his father were in such a low tone that I could barely catch any of it. Occasionally the cracked lips would give out a knowing chuckle and he would tap his nose as if he was worldly wise and Ken was naïve. After about twenty minutes we were dismissed and Ken was told to let his grandmother come in.

As Ken reached for the doorknob Denis snapped his thin neck back and said, "She's the one for you," before letting it loll back on his chest.

My relief when Ken picked up the string bag, after his grandmother had waddled disdainfully past me, was huge. I was filling our walk back to Ken's bedsit with nervous laughter and jokes which he was joining in with. It was as if we had been let out of a particularly nasty school detention. My car was parked outside Mum Williams's place as I had felt too nervous to drive.

"Come up for a bit of this bread and jam before you go?" he asked as we drew close to his bedsit.

"Why not!"

The bedsit was a lot cleaner than Ken's parental home, but it was tiny. The bed, wardrobe and table just about fitted in. There was a tiny sink next to a Baby Belling cooker, which consisted of one hot plate on top with a miniscule oven underneath. There was a cupboard and a drawer below the dolls-house-sized draining board. The whole "sink-draining board" had a piece of wood that could swing down on to it from a hook on the wall. This converted the area into either an ironing board or food preparation space.

After our jam and bread we headed for the bus back to Mum Williams' place. "Will you marry me?" Ken asked abruptly.

I was shocked. I hadn't even thought about it. I liked him a lot but did I love him? I was immensely flattered.

"Yes, but my mum won't let us 'til I'm 21."

"Doesn't matter. I'll wait."

We had known each other just over a week.

Chapter 16

I knew my parents would never give their consent to me marrying before the age of 21. My father behaved very strangely around any young man who showed even the vaguest interest in me, and my mother had become strongly attached to the money I put on the kitchen table every Friday afternoon. I wasn't bothered. I was in no rush to get married now that I was managing to keep Gerard's attentions at bay and had been promoted to the Xerox Department at work.

Jean Webb had been promoted to the Comptometer Department where they spent all day crunching numbers on the big brown mechanical computers. I had been quite interested in going there too, but in the end I was happy with my choice of the Xerox Department. I learned a fair amount about trouble-shooting photocopiers, and I had the bonus of meeting people from all the other departments in the bank. Every department needed photocopies and the people who brought the originals down to us always needed to stop and chat while the copies were going through, so I got to know all the inside gossip and which departments were fun to work in and which had problems.

One day the junior from Personnel came down looking like death warmed up.

"Have you heard?" she asked with a definite quiver in her voice.

"Heard what?"

"The Beatles have been killed in a plane crash."

I couldn't reply. I just stared at her red-rimmed eyes while praying she was going to say "April Fool" - in February. Slowly I copied her paperwork. She left without another word.

"I'm going to the loo," I muttered to my co-worker. I needed some privacy to deal with the huge lump that had stuck itself firmly in my throat and the pressure of tears behind my eyes. Pushing the bathroom door open I found there was not a single cubicle free and that many of the other girls were crouched around the walls sobbing. The depth of their grief added credence to the story and my resolve to be strong dissolved into an extremely soggy handkerchief.

Doubts began to creep in at lunchtime when we all dashed out to grab the latest newspapers and watch the flickering pictures through the windows of the television shop. Surely if *we* knew about these deaths, they would be on the news. We all walked back to work feeling exulted, but a little silly, and concentrated intently for the remainder of the day. We never found out how the rumour had begun. Hopefully the Longbank bosses didn't notice the serious lack of productivity that morning!

****

Ken always asked me to accompany him to his parents' house on Sunday afternoons and it was very rare that I could get out of it. There was nothing in that house that made things any lighter for me. Lillian, who for some reason was always called Queenie, was the sort of woman I could never warm to. She was a complete victim, convinced that her husband and son were both the very best at all things that anybody ever could be. She was also totally devoid of a sense of humour.

Every day Lillian would finish work at the factory before running to the chemist to get Denis's tablets, then running home to tend to him and cook for him. Her words to me were continually peppered with "Never": she "never had time to eat", "Denis never did anything wrong", "Ken never cried as a baby", she "never loved another man and never could", she had "never had a day without illness", had such poor circulation she could "never get warm" even in mid-summer. The fact that she was so weak made Ken even more attentive to her needs, yet she was destined to outlive everybody and only died a couple of years ago. I soon discovered that the mottled skin on the front of her legs was due to sitting so close to the electric fire that she constantly burnt them. It didn't matter how many people told her to move back, she insisted she had to be an inch away from it or she would "never be able to stand" as her joints would get too cold.

Denis's mother was the opposite of his wife. An old battle-axe who would not mince her words, however hurtful they might be. Every Sunday the last thing I would say before we knocked on the door was, "Please don't leave me with your grandmother. Please!" and Ken would promise not to, but it would always happen because Lillian would call him into the kitchen so she could give him some groceries, or Denis would want to see his wife and son together.

Ken's father came from quite good stock. Denis went to private schools but remained a disappointment to his parents. He was a sickly child who went on to become a sickly man and then develop paranoid schizophrenia. Denis's father was high up in Pearl Assurance and always wore a full suit with waistcoat and a pocket watch on a chain. He topped this off with a bowler hat and a rolled umbrella whenever he went to work. The Sharpe family had a huge house in East Croydon in which they rattled around with their only son until he got married and began his downward slide into madness.

The old lady was a mistress of speedy vitriol. She only needed Ken to be out of the room for a few seconds to get a week's worth of venom in before sitting back in her chair, clicking her teeth and oozing innocence when he returned.

"Would you mind not coming here on a Sunday," she once said the moment the sitting room door had been closed to keep the heat in. "I come here to see my son and he won't come into the room if *you* are here."

She knew full well that Ken insisted I came with him, but it wasn't so much the things she said as the inflection she gave them. She left me in no doubt that I was complete trash in her eyes. I was not worthy of being allowed anywhere near her beloved son or grandson, or the grimy house they lived in.

****

It was not surprising that I found it a double delight to escape from the Sharpes' house and return to Mum Williams for a cup of tea and some normality at the conclusion of my Sunday chore.

Nell would usually be reading the paper and fixated on the latest newsworthy evil, but at least that wasn't me. Derek Bentley had been posthumously pardoned in the Spring and his remains had been removed from Wandsworth Prison and buried in the family plot. Despite the whole family's enthusiasm for the announcement of the end of the death penalty, mainly due to their proximity to the Bentley family, serious doubts were worming in just a few short months later.

Ian Brady and Myra Hindley were on trial at Chester Assizes for the torture and murder of several children. "They should be strung up ..." Kath would cry at every fresh piece of information. But the story was so terrible that Nell would stop conversations about it and whisper, "Don't let the littleuns 'ear 'bout this ..." so everyone would stop talking. Although I was 19 years old she still thought I was too young to be party to the horrors of these particular crimes, and certainly my sisters didn't hear a sniff of it at the time.

There was a feeling among the public that justice could not be done because the pair could no longer be hung. Hindley's crimes were so wicked that for Mum Williams – the mother of all children, and a woman who could never bear to see them even slightly reprimanded – it was the sole sensationalist story that she was unable to read about. Any pages about the Moors Murders would be removed, tightly screwed up and used for the fire. It was too abhorrent to be allowed in the house.

While the trial was going on I developed bronchitis and pneumonia. My lungs had been my weak point ever since the childhood whooping cough had led to my continual eye problems. Even now that I was working and living with my parents, I ended up back at 21A West Street being nursed by Mum Williams. She was 79 years old and her legs gave her constant pain. She tottered painfully up and down the steep stairs to bring bottles of Lucozade and freshly baked scones into the middle bedroom. Every time she arrived she was dressed in a smile and a cheery word. She laundered my handkerchiefs and brought cool flannels when I had a fever, and she also kept the rest of her family fed and watered and still took in every pram that was parked inside her front gate.

Shortly after this, I had one of my last eye operations. The eye clinic was part of the old fever hospital. Ken had been quite good at visiting West Street when I was ill but he hated hospitals so his sole contribution this time was to run in, throw a bar of chocolate at me and say, "I love you, I'm going!" Still, it was better than nothing! At these times I missed not having a strong family. With Ken being an only child of a schizophrenic Dad and a mother who was as weird as you can possibly imagine, the big family thing was destined to never happen.

Despite Ken's dislike for the place, the hospital was lovely because it was beside a quiet industrial estate which backed onto open country. Squirrels used to hop into the ward because the nurses would open the doors into the garden. My eye lashes were cut off and there were stitches across my eyeball. However I was back to decent vision by the time England made the final of the World Cup. For the first time since the competition began in 1930 England had reached the end. The fact that they were pitched against West Germany at Wembley Stadium gave the game an added edge.

Although I didn't even like football I expected to watch the game either at 21A or through the window of the TV shop with crowds of other people. Ken and I were saving for our wedding and had virtually no money as Ken was still working in Clerkenwell getting his printing indentures. On the 30th July I let myself into Ken's bedsit to wait for him to get home from work and decide where we were going to watch the match.

The doorbell rang, so I went downstairs and opened the door to find Ken with a TV on his shoulder. Someone had lent it to him at work and he'd brought it all the way home on his shoulder on the train. Alan came down from the bedsit above and helped him to set it up, while his girlfriend, Valerie, and I set about turning the bed into a comfy sofa. With the curtains drawn, and taking it strictly in turn to hold up the aerial, we were ready for action when Bobby Moore led his team out onto the pitch.

When Germany took an early lead our spirits slumped a little, but we were on our feet in total elation as Geoff Hurst equalised minutes later. From then on we were leaping up and down every time England had possession of the ball. Our exuberance regularly upset the TV and the screen was covered in snow at vital moments however hard the aerial-holder tried to keep a clear signal.

"Hit it!" we all screamed at the TV minder as England took the lead in the second half when Martin Peters scored.

As Wolfgang Weber found the net 15 seconds from the final whistle we were sent into an uncontrollable frenzy, and when Hurst scored again in extra time we accidentally broke the bed!

Afterwards we celebrated big time – for us – by going to the off-licence and buying a bottle of cider.

****

My career at Longbank was going well and the bosses had decided it was worth teaching me to type and do shorthand. There was no way I was going to get close to the 120 words a minute needed to be a shorthand-typist, so I took a sideways step onto Dictaphone. This was before the time of cassette tapes and the bosses used to record their memos and letters onto big brown records, like LPs. The entire machine was brown, as were the headphones and under the desk there were pedals so the typist could stop and go backwards if they had missed what was said. Once we had finished a record, it would be put back into its sleeve so that notes could be written on it.

Once I had mastered typing and Dictaphone I chose to go into the Legal Department. It was a close run decision as I still fancied the Comptometer Department, not just because Jean Webb was still there, but because I liked dealing with numbers. However, the Legal Department was interesting because we had to chase people who didn't pay.

I worked for a man called Mr Glasscock. Naturally everybody took the mickey out of him, but actually he was lovely man although not very happy with the world. He didn't like many people and suffered from a speech impediment which made it impossible for him to dictate onto Dictaphone, so he was given a secretary and I was her under-secretary. His speech problems were the result of his time as a Japanese prisoner of war when his mouth was staked open which permanently split the inside.

I enjoyed working at Longbank and Nell was very proud that I was doing a desk job. It made me take pride in my appearance. Nobody was allowed to wear jeans and boys weren't allowed to grow beards or moustaches. If anyone arrived at work with a 5 o'clock shadow they were sent home and had their pay docked. Everyone signed in on arrival, and if you rushed the job and signed in beneath the line the head of Personnel, Mrs Voight, would personally haul you over the carpet.

Mrs Voight was a bit like Edwina Curry, but taller and very strong. She would tick you off if you were late and if you needed time off it was her you would have to beg. She dealt with everything, personally.

****

It wasn't until lunchtime on a Friday late in October that we heard about the landslide in Aberfan, South Wales. The shock at work was far worse than when we believed the Beatles had been killed. This time everyone, from the top brass to the part-time cleaners, knew it was true. By the time the long afternoon drew to a close we knew that most of the village schoolchildren were dead. Out of 131 children, only 25 were eventually dug out of the mud alive.

I walked down to 21A, as I would have done on any other Friday evening, but this time the streets seemed silent even though they were filled with people. Everything was hushed. It was as if the country was unable to breathe. The black and white TV screens in the electrical shop window flickered with pictures of hundreds of men digging with spades, or their bare hands. Those in suit jackets grappled with the mound of earth shoulder to shoulder with working men in flat caps, while everyone listened for the slighted sound of a voice. By the time the coal miners were called back from the pit, some of the women had no skin left on their hands from clawing at the black tidal wave that had engulfed their babies. Now the women were standing stock still, their bloodied hands hanging by their sides, waiting for a miracle.

Arriving at West Street, I witnessed Nell hobbling up and down the street, checking that all her neighbours' children were safe. There was no logical reason for her actions, but she was driven by pure impulse following the horror of what had happened.

"Even in the war we didn't 'ave such a tragedy," she muttered as I gently led her into the front room and warmed the pot for a cup of tea.

****

One day in the autumn of 1966 I was out at lunch with the girls from the bank when my eye began to itch and a little lump came up. Luckily my Head of Department knew about my eye history and told me to go straight up to the May Day hospital. The doctor found a stitch from many years before which had never dissolved and had worked its way to the fore just under my eyelid. He gave me some drops and told me to come back the following Tuesday. I went to work on Tuesday morning and then walked up the road to the hospital where they put other drops in my eye to freeze it completely before taking the eye out, again, and removing the stitch.

****

Sometimes we would all pile into whatever enormous car my father had at the time, and go down to see Peggy and Noel. Ken would come too and I would love the days we spent walking Uncle Noel's beagles over the fields with him, or visiting his workshop in New Haven where he kept his classic cars and a boat. Everyone liked Ken, especially as he asked thoughtful questions about record players, which was what Uncle Noel's latest business venture involved.

I say "everyone liked Ken", but my father was always ambivalent, or maybe it was jealousy. He certainly reacted very strangely and I could feel his eyes on us constantly.

In November Ken and I, my sisters and Flora were all in the kitchen together talking about the preparations we were making for Christmas. It was a jolly conversation with plenty of happy banter and as we left the room Ken put his arm round my mother's shoulders and gave her a friendly squeeze.

A few weeks later Ken and I had gone to our church group. We had gone with Bob, who used to be a lay preacher, and his wife Elizabeth, who was a very Christian woman. As it was Christmas we all got into singing carols and the evening speeded up more than we realised.

"I'll run you two home," Bob offered. It had already been arranged that Ken would be allowed to stay over – separate rooms of course.

We crept through the front door at 11pm. Flora was standing on the stairs despite the late hour.

"You've very late Margaret," and she hurried back up to her bed.

We switched the light on in the front room to be faced by a note in my father's writing propped up against the mantelpiece clock. "I am not impressed. See me in the morning. Dad."

The Christmas cheer had disappeared. In the morning we went down and stood in the little dining room while Gerard tore into us with every insult he could muster. Ken was no longer welcome at my parents' house and was not to come unless he was specifically invited. If he was allowed through the front door he was not allowed to sit next to me.

Once Ken had left my parents really got into the swing of things.

"Your mother has told me that Ken touches her inappropriately. We don't know how you could think of marrying a man like that! Imagine how your children might turn out!"

Chapter 17

My parents suddenly moved from the big corner house in Hedley Drive to a flat in Old Coulsdon. By this time Tina had turned 13 and had moved in with us – ready for the moment she became 14 and could be sent out to work. For the first time ever the house at Hedley Drive had a full quota of occupants with no need to lie about us being at boarding school, so I'm not sure why they were suddenly moved on.

The new apartment had three bedrooms, so Christine and Tina had to share, while I had the box room, which, thankfully, was big enough for my furniture. Although all of us, apart from Christine, were paying to live there, we still weren't given a key to the door so we had to make sure one of our parents was in before arriving back, and that we were home before they went to bed.

All achievement hopes were pinned on Christine. There was no doubt that she was academically bright, so she was allowed to remain at school as it was thought she would go to university. In the end she went to teacher training college instead, but despite their pride in her, neither Gerard nor Flora paid anything towards her accommodation or other costs during her studies.

Flora was even stricter about money with Tina than she had been with me. If there was even the sniff of a rise, Tina would have to pay more. It was common for our mother to go into Tina's room at 5am on a Saturday morning to shake her awake and say, "Don't go out without leaving my money in the morning!"

Despite this, Tina sent funds to Christine continually to keep her at college. I have to admit that my contributions were more sporadic as, by the time she went, I was already married and had a home of my own to run. Christine still thanks her lucky stars for her younger sister without whom, she says, she would have literally starved at that time.

Before that, though, life rolled on at the flat and I eased my way closer to 21 and the age of freedom.

Although Ken and I had agreed to get engaged when I was 19, we didn't buy a ring until two years later. We chose one at the jewellers, Ernest Jones, where you could pay it off in instalments. We decided our official engagement would be at Easter 1967 as I would be 21 the following September. We chose Easter because we would both have a couple of days off work and we wanted to have a bit of a celebration with our friends and a special dinner at the Savoy in London.

"We're getting engaged in April," I said to my mother one day, not that she was particularly interested!

As it turned out Easter was three weeks earlier than the previous year. We realised this in January so I changed my announcement to, "We're getting engaged in March" – engaged, that is, not married, we would still be getting married as soon as possible after I turned 21. However, this three week change let to a barrage of accusations from my parents.

"We're not surprised you're pregnant, you always were loose!" … "The shame you bring on this family, I only hope it doesn't rub off on your younger sisters!" … "He'll probably run off before you get to the church now he's tasted all the fruit!"

I would walk down the aisle a virgin, never having done anything more than cuddle and kiss with anyone, except for what was forced upon me by the father who was now accusing me of being an untrustworthy little bitch.

Unsurprisingly we celebrated our engagement at Mum Williams' house and I stayed there on the Thursday night and for all of Good Friday. On Saturday morning I went to have my hair done before catching the bus up Old Coulsdon to get ready for our date at the Savoy that evening. The front door was open and my mother was coming out.

"Oh come on Margaret, I'm trying to catch the next bus, I thought you'd be home earlier than this!"

I stuck my hand out as I walked towards her to show off my engagement rock, which I absolutely loved. She wrinkled her nose.

"Hmmm, couldn't he have done any better than that? There's a parcel for you on the kitchen table," and with that she was trotting off in the direction of the bus stop.

Usually anything valuable would get my mother's covetous side going, so the fact that she was so dismissive stung more than I expected. I made my way to the kitchen hoping for a pleasant surprise to cheer me up. On the table was a small parcel wrapped in brown paper. Inside was a card, a packet of cigarettes – for Ken – and two Irish linen pillow cases. They hadn't exactly broken the bank, but at least they had acknowledged the occasion. I opened the card.

"*To Margaret and Ken, best wishes, Mr and Mrs O'Callaghan.*"

****

As the wedding drew closer there was a slight thawing in my parents' treatment of Ken. He was allowed to pick me up from the house and could come in for a brief amount of time if we had to wait for a bus. However, if we were sitting together and Gerard entered the room we would separate, we certainly couldn't hold hands or anything like that. My father would install himself in his chair and drum the fingers of his non-smoking hand, the muscles of his chin constantly flexing with the gritted teeth inside. The atmosphere crackled and the wait for the bus seemed suddenly endless.

Despite my continued slim waistline neither of them apologised for their accusations of pregnancy. They considered they had been right all along but I had just got rid of it. There is no effective way of fighting these manufactured phantom rumours. Whatever I said they would always believe their fabrications. So I said nothing.

Our marriage was booked for the 14th of September, nine days after my 21st birthday. On Monday 14th of August I was called to the telephone at work, it was Ken.

"Dad's gone into the Mayday on Open Order. Can you come?"

I'd done the obligatory visit to Ken's home just the day before, but Open Order was when death was imminent and meant that anyone could visit the patient at any time. Although I wanted to make an excuse of work, my boss told me that I must go.

"You might be a bit shocked," Ken said as he met me in the corridor. Denis was dying of kidney failure from all the poisons he put into his blood. Throughout his illness he had either not taken the tablets he needed, or tipped whole bottles down himself all at once.

I walked into the room holding Ken's hand. The old man had lost control of his limbs which were shooting out all over the place. His tongue lolled out of his mouth. Suddenly he jolted upright and gave a ghastly groan. Lillian was thrown off from where she had been bending over him, sobbing, "My Denis, oh my Denis …" The macabre scene left me rooted to the floor in horror until Lillian broke the spell by asking me to go outside so that Ken and her could say goodbye together. It was the sole thing she did for me for which I will always be grateful. Ken didn't want me to leave, but this time I was in complete agreement with my future mother-in-law.

A short time later they emerged from behind the curtain. Lillian was completely distraught. I had imagined she would feel some kind of relief after decades of living on her nerves with someone so seriously ill. How wrong I was! She donned her widow's weeds and never removed them again, either mentally or physically.

In addition to our wedding preparations there was now a funeral to sort out. I met Ken straight from work one evening.

"We're going round to see Dad."

"All right, I'll wait here."

"Oh no, I really want you to come."

"I don't really want to Ken, I've never seen a dead person and I'm sure it's better if you just go with your Mum. I didn't really know him ..."

"Please come. For me. Mum will be very upset if you don't."

"All right, but you won't leave me will you? Promise you won't leave me."

The undertaker was quite tall with carefully combed white hair. He shook our hands as we walked through the door and tried to console Lillian, speaking in the very quiet and measured way they do in funeral parlours.

"He's in one of our chapels down here," he said, wafting us down the corridor past other closed doors. I imagined the stiff corpses lying in each of them until he slid back the entrance and ushered us inside. There was barely room to walk around the coffin. A tiny shelf on the wall housed a cross and two candles with a little embroidered drape and braiding. That was all there was to create the idea of a chapel. I clung to Ken for dear life, trying to avoid looking at the old man. Lillian bent over him on the opposite side. She suddenly straightened up and whispered something to the undertaker.

"Of course, of course," he murmured, sliding the door open and then closed behind him as he left the room.

A few minutes later he returned with a huge pair of scissors. She took them from him while my petrified gaze was glued to her mottled hand as it slowly cut off a large chunk of wispy grey hair.

****

It was lucky I'm pretty good at budgeting as our wedding, on top of the housekeeping that I paid my parents, was a serious expense. Not only did we have to pay for the church, flowers, and honeymoon, but, in addition to my dress, my mother expected me to buy her an outfit as well.

Dressing Flora for a wedding, especially one where Peggy and Noel would be present, didn't come cheap – after all, there should be no doubt about who was the star of the show! – the handbag and shoes had to match the outfit and all of them must be of the latest design.

However, the 5th of September was *my* day, my twenty-first, a time to be spoilt a little. As tradition had it that almost everybody would stop giving presents after you "came of age" it was customary for twenty-first gifts to be generous. Women usually received silver-backed dressing table sets or pieces of jewellery from their family.

I didn't expect anything so grand, although Ivy gave me a dressing table set, the mirror was backed in blue enamel and the comb and brush were edged in silver, it was beautiful. But what I really wanted was a vanity case. I kept on and on about it to my parents. I envisaged taking it on my honeymoon, carefully locked with its own little key, it's satin pockets filled with my makeup and a polished mirror on the inside of the lid.

As I left for work that Tuesday morning my mother handed me a grey paper bag with the distinctive green logo of Marks & Spencer. It certainly wasn't big enough for a vanity case.

"Happy Birthday. I didn't have time to write a card."

The bag contained two pairs of cotton airtex knickers. In white.

After work Ken and I strolled down to 21A. At over 80 years old, Mum Williams was creaking from kitchen to front room, round and round with plates of sandwiches, scones, jam, butter, and finally, a birthday cake. Once her family had feasted and she was free to collapse onto the sofa, she pulled out a large wrapped present that had been hidden behind it.

"'ere you go Margy…" as Hilda, Kath and the others smiled at me and I felt the deep warmth of my family of women.

I carefully removed the paper, folding it to save for later, and tried to stop my eyes from welling over as I took out the beautiful vanity case.

****

A couple of days later I had to go and have a last word with the caterers after work and missed my bus home. I should have arrived by 10.30.

"I'll come in and explain what happened," Ken said as we walked up the driveway at 11.20.

My father was striding up and down outside the front door, already seething with indignation.

"What time do you call this? I can only imagine what you've been doing out at this time of night! No better than a street walker…"

****

My wedding day dawned and my father wasn't well. He couldn't breathe. My mother had her handbag on her arm, "If you want something to eat you'll have to get it yourself, I'm off to the hairdressers."

I made Christine and Tina scrambled egg on toast while my father smoked his way through another half a packet of cigarettes before taking the three of us to the hair salon too. On the way we took in his shoes to be mended. Once we had been washed, curled and primped he drove us home via a man's clothing shop where he went in to buy a suit and a black umbrella as the skies were already darkening.

We had ordered two big modern V6 cars to take us to the church, one for my mother, sisters and Peggy, and the other for my father and I. As wedding dresses don't usually have pockets, I gave my father an envelope with 20 guineas in it. The cars only cost ten pounds so there would be plenty of money left over for our honeymoon. As the first black car swept out of the drive I was left standing in the front room with Uncle Noel. He took me by the hand.

"You look absolutely beautiful."

My eyes filled with tears, "Do you know Uncle Noel, I would rather it was you giving me away today."

It was my last appeal, but of course it was impossible. Noel left and the old man and I went down to the car. By the time we arrived at the church the heavens had opened. My father unrolled his new umbrella and held it over me as I walked up the pathway. Large black drops of fresh dye rolled off it onto my white dress. I was destined to get married looking like a Dalmatian!

The deed was done. The photos taken. I stood as far away from him as I could while he hid his nicotine brown fingers in the sleeves of his jacket.

"We're going now, can I have the envelope please."

He handed me a crumpled, empty bit of paper. "Where's the change?"

"I gave it to the drivers as a tip. You wouldn't want us to look cheap!"

It was a large amount of money, but, at the time it wasn't my first priority.

I was terrified. I had already experienced far too much to believe that sex would be enjoyable. It's like the second time you go to the dentist when you had a tooth out on the first visit, you know what you're in for, and you know that you'll hate it.

Chapter 18

Arriving back from our honeymoon we were very excited to be moving into our own place. I went to the telephone box to make an arrangement to go and collect my things – obviously I couldn't have just turned up at their house without an appointment!

"Ken says we can borrow a van to collect my bedroom furniture…"

"I didn't think you'd be wanting that old stuff," Flora replied. "You should 'ave said. I sold it while you were away enjoying yourselves. There's some of your clothes and things still around if you want them."

She never mentioned how much she got for the furniture that I had spent over a year paying off on hire purchase! Still I didn't want Mum to spoil my mood.

"Once we're settled into our new place we'll have you and the girls round for dinner."

So we did. There was a little butchers around the corner from our flat and a host of other grocers shops close by. With Ken's wage and the good pay packet I was now on at Longbank I ended up having a whole five pounds a week for housekeeping. It seemed like a fortune! We even had enough money to eat out at one of the nearby Italian or Greek restaurants on a Friday night.

I cooked my best meal for my sisters and parents, and made the flat look as nice as possible. Ken was trying to be a perfect host to Flora and Gerard whilst I finished off in the kitchen. Christine came in. She had just turned 15 and had been to her first school dance the week before. She stood close to me as I stirred the soup, leaning in to whisper.

"Dad went mad at me after the dance. He said afterwards it was because of you."

"I don't see how, seeing as I don't even live there any longer!"

"George walked me home after the dance, just to be polite, I wasn't doing anything wrong. But Dad must have been behind the front door as I came up the path 'cos when I opened it he sprang out and grabbed me. He was grinding his teeth and growling "Get in!" at me, and then he was really rude to George. I don't know what he's going to tell the others in our class. It was so embarrassing and horrible."

"So how was all of that my fault?"

"He said they believed you were going to be a prostitute when you were 15 and they didn't want me going the same way."

The only strange thing about this conversation was that it had happened to Christine, had it been Tina or me his behaviour would have been completely normal. It was the only time I know of that she had a run in with him.

The meal was tense, as I should have predicted, and then Flora started on about something which developed into a big argument. As she left, puffed up with righteous indignation, she turned round and said, "Anyway, I've never been to such a horrible wedding as yours!"

It was definitely time for me to start making my new life and leave the old one firmly in the past.

****

The area we had moved into was pleasant enough. One of our neighbours was a prison guard who used to drive the Kray twins back and forth between prison and the Old Bailey. He had to make his way through the huge crowds that gathered daily outside the courthouse and there was a constant worry that some fellow gangsters would hatch a plan to break them out and they would never serve their sentences. Our neighbour used to transport them in under eight minutes, which was some kind of record. Because of his speed, and the perceived danger of his task, he was awarded the CBE a few years later, which, among other things, allowed his children to get married in the crypt at St Paul's cathedral, even though he was the same as you or I.

We settled into married life. Ken's mum came round regularly on Sundays and Wednesdays, yet somehow I felt in limbo now that I no longer belonged at Mum William's house and I certainly couldn't have gone round to my parents' place. I visited 21A sometimes to take Nell custard tarts and have a chat, but it wasn't nearly as regular as before. I had our own dinner to cook and chores to do after work.

One time when I went round Mum Williams asked me to get the pedal organ valued. It had stood in her old bedroom with all her other treasures for my entire life, but it had been many years since we had used it to sing carols around. I found a man who was prepared to buy it for 100 guineas, which I thought sounded all right, especially as I wasn't sure it was still in working order.

"That's daylight robbery!" Nell exploded, "We won't 'ave that thieving bastard back round 'ere."

So we didn't.

Despite the fact that Ken's mum was now a free woman and wasn't very old, she still completely refused to spend a single night away from the house. She claimed that as she had promised Denis never to stop out, she had to go back there come hell or high water. There were evenings when the rain was coming down in sheets and bouncing up to your knees off the pavement while the thunder and lightning raged above, and she would still insist that Ken had to walk her to her cold empty house rather than stay over with us!

Every year after Denis died, the last birthday card and anniversary card would come out on the appropriate dates and be propped up on the mantelpiece for a week or so before being carefully put away again. Lillian never moved Denis's photograph, and we would frequently find her sitting knitting, and crying, with the television on and a photograph of her with Denis next to her. For quite a few years, every time her birthday came round she would take money that was in the pockets of his grimy old dressing gown, which still hung on the bedroom door, and go and buy herself a present. Then she would carefully put the receipt in the dressing gown pocket.

Until the money ran out we always heard about what "Denis bought me for my birthday this year …"

****

Although Ken and I were good friends, and had our weird upbringings in common, the first few years of married life were not easy for me and things got worse before they got better. For many years I had a patch of eczema just above the centre of my bottom. I would scratch it until it bled, it would drive me mad, yet often there was nothing to see. I think it was probably a nervous thing from direct association with my father.

Then Ken and I fell out big time on the evening when I went out to a work's do with the girl who lived next door. We used to have a loft in our apartment. It was so large that we put a ping-pong table up there and friends used to come round and play table-tennis. So, when we went out it made sense for my neighbour's husband to come round for a few games whilst we were away.

When we arrived home they weren't in the attic but were watching something on television. TV at the end of the 1960s was pretty tame compared to today, so it can't have been really bad but it did involve women undressing and they were sitting their looking at it.

Something inside me snapped. From that minute on I wouldn't let Ken near me. He was frustrated because he thought he had done something wrong, but whenever he asked me I just said, "No, it's nothing." I went into a deep depression and began to get migraines that were so bad that I would often pass out. As we were on the top floor, I couldn't even go down to answer the doorbell if I had a migraine brewing as I had collapsed going back up a couple of times. I went to the doctor and he thought it was the migraines that were making me depressed and gave me some pills which just knocked me out. My job was beginning to be in jeopardy, so Ken insisted I went back to the doctor to see what else he might have in his arsenal.

"I'm not sleeping, I'm not feeling any better, my husband and I have started to have arguments and feel bad towards each other," I mumbled.

"Right, talk me through this. Was there a definite starting point?"

"No, I just flipped when I came home and Ken and Alan from next-door were watching something on the television that involved women taking their clothes off."

"Is there anything wrong with your married sexual life," he asked.

"No."

But eventually we got around to my father and the abuse and I remember getting terribly upset while I told him because he was the first person I had told since Peggy when I was a lot younger.

This doctor was from Thornton Heath and, even though it was on the National Health, he definitely wasn't constrained by ten minute appointment slots. Once I had calmed down he took me out to the old records room where they used to keep huge filing cabinets with all the information about patients stored in brown envelopes.

"All these are my patients. At least fifty per cent of them have had the same sort of experience as you. You are not to think that you are the only one. We can get you through this."

I talked and talked to this kindly man, and then he sent me home to tell Ken.

Telling Ken was quite difficult for me and I certainly didn't give him any details, I just said my father did bad things to me.

He didn't really react. I didn't expect lashings of sympathy, after all we had been going through quite a rough time, but I thought he might be indignant, he could have said "How dare he!" and advise me not to see my father again. He didn't though.

"Now we've got this out in the open, I understand, you have got to know that you can tell me anything, we are husband and wife, I love you, you love me," and that was it.

After I told Ken I expected him to be a little different towards my parents, yet on the rare occasions when they came over, although I wouldn't go downstairs to say goodbye, he would, and I would watch him out of the window shaking my father's hand and slapping him on the back. To me it seemed so disloyal. I buried my feelings because I didn't want to put a further rift in our marriage. I knew Ken was always outgoing with everybody. It was part of his charm. He was a very intelligent man, but I lost some respect for him after that.

The doctor was as good as his word and I did go to counseling, all sorts of counseling, off and on over the years. Some of it was a bit wacky, some quite helpful. The one thing counseling taught me is that you can't do anything about anyone else, you can only deal with yourself. To be honest I don't think you ever get over being messed about with. They call you an "abuse survivor", but I believe everybody has their problems. When you look at someone you may think "My god, she's got everything," but it's probably not true. Still, I always wonder if I would have been a better person if my father had left me alone. "Better" is the wrong word, perhaps I mean "different". I think I would have been stronger and achieved more. Although I think of myself as a strong person, and my friends would agree, I'm always haunted by the thought that, if I really were strong, I would have stopped it.

Logically, I know I was a child, and that an adult male versus a female child is the most uneven of relationships when it comes to power, but when it's you yourself there's no hard black line in your life when you move from child to adult and so the questions go round and round in my head, "Could I have stopped him that time … or this time … Could I have stood up for myself and made myself proud rather than ashamed?"

What haunts any of us is rarely rational.

Chapter 19

And then I got pregnant - properly pregnant this time. I had undergone a miscarriage about a year after we married.

Once my belly started to swell and I could feel the new life struggling inside me I began to panic about having a girl. I prayed for a boy. I thought I would never be able to relax if I had a girl. I would be constantly worried that all men were like my father and that Ken would abuse her. I brooded on what Auntie Peggy had said about sexual interference being part of normal family life. I didn't care what anybody else said was "normal" - even if it was my lovely Aunt – nobody was going to touch my child!

Even before I gave birth my protective instinct towards my baby was firing on all cylinders. It was stoked daily, by fear. If I had a girl would I be able to watch her every minute? Would I definitely know if anyone had touched her? Would she have the confidence in me, that I never had in my own mother, to tell me if someone frightened her? Were all men the same?

I prayed for a boy even harder.

****

By this time Marjory and Charlie were no longer living a couple of doors down from 21A. They had bought the whole of the big house where Ivy and Cliff lived on the ground floor. Ivy and Cliff were now renting their garden apartment from their sister and brother-in-law, so there were two reasons for me to walk over Duppus Hill for a visit.

The move turned out to have been a lucky one for Ivy because Cliff suddenly got taken into hospital. Ivy had always been my favourite of the sisters. If she hadn't got asthma she would have been a fantastic mum, and Cliff would have made a great dad. Both Cliff and Charlie had huge amounts of energy, always racing us into the freezing sea when we went to the beach, or making us go-karts out of orange boxes and pram wheels, or taking us up to the aerodrome to learn about aviation. They weren't the slipper-and-pipe type of men, there was always something going on and they were in the middle of it.

So it was a shock for the whole family when Cliff was taken into St Helier Hospital in Sutton. Still, nobody thought there could be much wrong in a man who was so young and active.

We were wrong. Ivy was told that there was a whole bunch of vital things wrong with Cliff and his chances of survival were negligible.

"We don't want him to know," Ivy said to me after she tearfully explained the situation. I went to the hospital to visit him with a few other people. Cliff lifted his head up and looked around the room.

"What's everybody doing here? Is there something really bad going on?"

So we joked with him and told him it was just because we had nothing better to do on a rainy afternoon, and he laughed and called us a load of devils and told us he'd get his own back once he got out of there.

But he didn't. He was only 48 when he died.

"Who'd'ave known Cliff 'ad all those things wrong with 'im!" Mum Williams said when it was all over.

Ivy never married again. Cliff had been the love of her life and she was content to remain in their apartment with her sister and brother-in-law upstairs, but it was a sad time for the family which, for a while, brought us all back together again.

****

Despite her great age, Nell was still the matriarch and the rules against Cyril using the front door or the front room, remained in force. However, she had found it impossible to ban him from keeping his dog in the old shop. The dog was left there when Cyril went to work and one of the women was meant to let it out to pee at regular intervals. As Kath and Hilda were also at work, most of the time the task fell to Mum Williams. From the puppy it swiftly became a huge Alsatian which was completely untrained and nothing like the docile dogs we had owned when I was a child.

Mum Williams was bowled over by Cyril's dog on several occasions and everyone was nervous around it. Cyril, however, found the savage element appealing, in the same way he had done with the crocodile. The house quickly became smelly and the shop was humming. As far as Nell's meticulous hygiene standards were concerned, Cyril's dog was causing them to slide and she was no longer physically strong enough to fight against it. Kath's distain for Cyril, and baiting of Hilda, rose to new, angry, levels.

****

Obvious pregnancy obliged women to leave work in the early 1970s and I was very sorry to leave Longbank, but it couldn't be helped. Ken's work, however, was picking up. He had been advised to change companies after he finished his print apprenticeship as everyone said "Don't stay on where you've done your apprenticeship or they will always look upon you as the junior". Ken moved from Clerkenwell to Southwark where there was a general printing company.

With no job I had more time to spend at 21A and to occasionally see my mother. Despite my expanding waistline, any baby talk came straight back to Flora's own childbirth experiences, "When I gave birth to Margaret … to this day I don't know how I'm still here …" She didn't inspire me with confidence for what was ahead! She certainly wouldn't be around to put cool flannels on my forehead or hold my hand!

It was chilly in early December, but I was restless and anxious to know my fate – did I have a daughter or a son? I decided to take some custard tarts down to Mum Williams to occupy my mind while Ken was away at work. I walked all the way from Thornton Heath through into South Croydon, stopping at the bakery on the way. As my enormous tummy preceded me into the front room Kath gasped.

"Look at the size of 'er Mum! She's never going to get into a pair of 'ot-pants!"

"Ooo my gawd!" Nell cried out, clasping her gnarled fingers to her face as she hobbled out of the kitchen and caught sight of me. "When's that baby due?"

"About three days ago, Mum." I said, waving the bag of custard tarts at her.

"You get yourself sat down right now! You shouldn't 'ave come out like that! You should 'ave been in bed all this week, an' the one before by the looks of you! Don't you know nuffink 'bout 'aving babies? You's meant to rest before, not go striding over 'alf the country!"

"I've got to walk back yet!" I said with a wink to Kath as I took a poke at Mum's Victorian ideas, which were always set in stone.

"You'll do no such thing! I couldn't 'ave it on my conscience if somefink 'appened to your beautiful baby. Kath'll run you 'ome. You're not walking anywhere else until that baby's three weeks into weening. You 'ear me!"

****

On the 11th December 1970 I got to meet my precious daughter and, after all my months of worrying and praying for a different outcome, nothing could have prepared me for the ocean of love I felt from the second I first saw her.

My parents were living about 500 yards from the May Day hospital and only half a mile from where Ken and I had now moved to in Bencham Lane, but Flora didn't "have time" to pop in and see her first grandchild for more than three weeks.

When I left hospital I insisted we went home via 21A even though it was out of our way. I knew Mum Williams would be so happy to see her first "great-grandchild" – as she would consider Teresa – but I was unprepared for how Kath reacted.

"Oh Mum, look at 'er, she's like the sweetest little doll!"

Stern Kath, who would put mustard in our mouths and hold us up to the undertaker's window to scare us, was transformed into a soggy heap of adoration! She couldn't keep her eyes off Teresa, and would be the first to hold out her arms to take her when I parked the pram outside. She would walk around the front room with Teresa, talking to her and stroking her soft downy head. For Kath, nothing was too much trouble where my baby was concerned.

My mother was somewhat different, which I found even more incomprehensible now that I had given birth myself and felt such an overwhelming bond with my child. She did say Teresa was "very nice" when she finally saw her, but she didn't buy anything for her or cuddle her. She didn't spend time with us and she was the last person on earth we would have asked to babysit. She was even worse than Lillian – and we had to show her where the light switches were and how to work the kettle every time we left the house for an hour, so Ken's mum wouldn't have been tough to beat!

Now that I had a baby of my own, I became increasingly angry with my mother for her complete lack of maternal instinct. I couldn't understand how she could just give her babies away, time and time again. I would look at childhood pictures of the three of us, all done up beautifully in our white buckskin shoes and lacy socks, and a disbelieving rage would well up inside me. How could anyone not have loved us? How could our parents not have been proud of the family they had created? Thank god for the quiet saints of the world like Nell. What on earth would have happened to us without her enduring care? Flora was so incredibly cold I would be more likely to talk to somebody at the bus stop than my mother if I needed advice or support.

Flora didn't understand my frustration at all, which made me even angrier. I never let rip at her, but I would certainly become lippy now that I had my own family. Flora was always comparing us, unfavourably, with other people's daughters.

"Mrs Jones's daughter bought her a new television set, I told her my daughters would never do something like that for me. I don't know why my children are so ungenerous, but there you are …"

"Probably because you did absolutely nothing for us!"

"How can you be so ungrateful after all we've given you," she'd say, her pitch rising. "I don't know why you are always so angry with us Margaret!" so I'd shrug and leave. It was impossible for me to respect either of them.

****

I was determined to enjoy every minute of Teresa's babyhood, which was just as well as it turned out to be my only chance at having a baby. I suffered an ectopic pregnancy the following year.

We organised a christening three months after Teresa was born at St Andrews, where Ken and I had got married. Everyone was invited back to our house but only Marjory and Charlie could come from the 21A family because of Mum William's legs and other things. My sisters were both godmothers and we had a cine film taken to record the big event.

Philip was there with his wife, Brenda. They had a nine month old boy who was simply huge. He was crawling around the floor, in and out of the legs of the guests, a hand shooting out regularly to grab something off the coffee tables.

"Can he eat that?" I said, nudging Philip when I saw him cramming a whole sausage in his mouth.

"Don't worry, as long as it's dead, he'll eat it!"

I began to be glad that I hadn't had a boy after all!

The christening had been a massive chore to undertake and cater for mainly because the country had changed to decimal currency the month beforehand. There were charts up everywhere to help people convert old prices into new, but the old ways of 12 pence to the shilling and 24 shillings to the pound were deeply entrenched, so that even though a system of 100 pence to the pound seemed so much simpler, people struggled. All the elderly shop keepers in our area were floundering to remember prices in the new money, let alone add them up!

If, on top of the staff problems, you got an old lady in front of you in the queue, it would take ages for her to work out what all the coins and notes were and what combinations she needed to pay her bill. For the first year it seemed to take hours to do the shopping – there were still very few supermarkets about – and if you also had a baby in a pram there was a fifty per cent chance that by the time you arrived at the front of the queue the little one would be balling its head off and throwing everything out of the pram due to the lengthy wait.

****

We decided I should look for a job shortly after Teresa was born because the printing industry was going through a difficult period. Ken was good at his job but all the unions were on the rise and nobody dared to fall foul of them. It didn't matter how skilled and diligent you were, or how sloppy the work of some of your peers, if you were last in then you were first out. As Ken had changed companies after his apprenticeship was completed, he was last in, so we were concerned. We had experienced an expensive time with the birth and christening - the luxury of not working wouldn't pay the rent. Obviously I couldn't go back to Longbank as I could only work when Ken was at home, or at a job to which I could take Teresa. I found Tupperware.

Tupperware was an American company which had developed plastic containers for keeping food fresh in the home. They were famous for their patented "burping seal" which was meant to show that freshness was sealed in! Tupperware wasn't sold in shops but was obtained from representatives who convinced local housewives to host a party, at which all their friends would be introduced to the wonders of Tupperware. Potential hostesses were frequently persuaded to give a party by a carrot – a real orange one – which they were asked to put in a Tupperware box. Through this they became part of a "scientific experiment". After a week they had to compare the freshness of the Tupperware carrot with those not given the airtight treatment, often this led to the birth of a new Tupperware party. Kerching!

I began knocking on doors and getting women to do the carrot test, but was soon made a manager and had the job of recruiting my own team. I wasn't doing parties every night but I still made a decent amount of commission. Once I was a manager I would look out for hostesses or guests who seemed like they could sell and then ask them if they had ever thought of doing parties themselves. If they wanted to sign up I would go out during the day to train them and set them up. Luckily Teresa was a good baby and it was never a problem to take her along with me, together with all the rest of the paraphernalia, even if I had to go on the bus.

Ken and I slowly got back on our financial feet. The mood in the country was buoyant despite the rising Union militancy and in October the UK joined the European Economic Community, forerunner of the EU.

By the following year I was doing so well at Tupperware that they gave me a company car. It was a gold Vauxhall Viva which only had four miles on the clock when it was delivered. The shiny motor sitting outside our flat was the impetus necessary for Ken to learn to drive. We were more settled by this time. Ken had a job near Hatton Gardens, but as he finished at 4.30am and the trains didn't start running until 6am, I would get up at night to go and pick him up. I could strap Teresa's cot into the back seat and she would never stir, so long as I fed her when we got home. Then we would all go back to bed together.

Life was good and we decided it was time we moved out of rented accommodation and get onto the property ladder. There was one problem. Ken was great at his job, marvellous with music, had the memory of an elephant, took fantastic care of me and Teresa, but … he didn't know one end of a screwdriver from the other. Consequently, we needed a house that was not a "project".

We went to view a little two-up-two-down in Gloucester Road with our nextdoor neighbour, Alan. I hated the house from the moment we walked in. There was an inside bathroom, but no inside toilet.

"Not to worry," Alan chirped, "that's an easy thing to sort out."

"Not for us it isn't!" I said, but Ken was on a testosterone ride with his mate and reality was thrown out of the ill-fitting windows.

"I'll be all right Marg, I'll fix that …"

The house was on the market for two thousand seven hundred and fifty pounds so we were getting a local council mortgage, but we were still a little bit short. I reckoned there was no chance we would get the place and that I could stop making waves about the building's shortcomings because it wasn't going to happen anyway.

"I think I'll go and see the seller in case he'll drop the price a bit."

"All right," I said feeling very confident that he wouldn't.

"We've got it" Ken said an hour later, swinging me around by my waist in glee. There wasn't any point in complaining now.

We bought the house and moved in on a Thursday. The following Monday Ken came home a broken man. He'd been made redundant. It was another case of last man in, first man out, but this time we had a mortgage, a baby and no savings, having spent every penny on moving and furnishing our new home.

Chapter 20

Ken's work was covered by the National Graphical Association (NGA) and so he was unable to claim the dole. Like his fellow journeymen, he paid dues to the Father of the Chapel, whose office was in Ludgate Hill. To prove that he wasn't working, Ken had to cycle over to Ludgate Hill, as we had no money for the bus. Once there, he would sign a book before going through into the next room to sign onto a Positions List. The Chapel would take the first six names off the top of the list and send them along for an interview for any jobs that were going.

The main way of supporting the men who had lost their job was to find them work, but we were given a pound here and there from the Chapel, when things were getting really tight.

All our excitement at buying our own house had turned to strife and the country as a whole seemed to be seething with dissatisfaction. The unions had been wrestling with the government and the miners were already striking regularly. Things became so bad that in February 1972 electricity was rationed, and then the dock strikes began which made things even worse.

I walked over to see Mum Williams one afternoon and make sure she was all right. She had dug out all her candles and appeared to believe she was back in the war, fighting the Jerries instead of the TUC. The newspaper was on the front room table as usual.

"Hey Mum, have you seen this, it says we have to wrap you in it!"

"What you on about Margy!" She lurched towards me on her painfully bandy legs, a slopping cup of tea in each hand and her old eyes laughing.

"Look Mum! "How to care for the elderly: Put newspaper pages between the bed blankets of elderly to keep them warm when the house heating has been cut off …"

"Ain't nobody goin' to cover me in a load of noosprint, I've got me pride! 'Ow's Ken doin?"

"Not so good Mum …"

"'E's a clever man, 'e'll get somefink Margy, mark my words it'll work out."

But for a long time it didn't.

Tupperware was our saviour during this period, although I couldn't commit to more work in case Ken was picked from the Positions List. He got the odd day here and there. Then the three-day week was brought in due to the lack of coal, oil and electricity and prices skyrocketed in the shops at just the time we didn't have two beans to rub together.

****

"I've got a job, but it's holiday cover," Ken announced one day after finally being sent for an interview.

"How long's it for?"

"Only a fortnight, but it's on a paper."

Holiday cover jobs on newspapers were coveted as it was known that if you did a good job they would ask you back rather than go through the Chapel again. Unfortunately, however, we were not going to see any money from Ken's work for a while longer.

Colin was Ken's friend who had acted as Best Man at our wedding. He was still single and could smell food from a mile away. Whenever I was making dinner I subconsciously made enough for Colin as, like as not, he would be at the door by the time the plates hit the table, especially at the weekends.

As usual we were chatting and playing dominoes with Colin until the early hours. At 3.30am we quietly let Colin out of the front door before creeping wearily up to bed ourselves. My neighbour had asked me to pay her milk bill for her as she was going away for the weekend and I had put the envelope with her money in it behind the clock that Mum Williams gave us as a wedding present. Ken's jacket, with his first pay packet in the inside pocket, was hanging on the back of the chair.

The sash window in our front room hadn't opened since the day we bought the place, which hadn't bothered us as it was too cold to have it open most of the time. When we came downstairs the following morning we found the window wide open and Ken's jacket and the envelope gone. Our tiny front garden was behind a tall hedge so nobody would have seen anyone prising the sash up from the street. Some friends brought round a big food parcel to keep us – and Colin – going. Luckily Ken's determination to make a good impression at the *Daily Telegraph* paid off. He was asked back, then asked to stay on again, then asked to work nights and finally given a permanent job which allowed him to stay with the newspaper for many years.

We could breathe again.

****

"There's a jazz band playing in the town at that place that has a family room, fancy going?" Ken asked one Sunday when I was about 25. Ken loved all music, even modern jazz which I'm not particularly keen on. He got me to love jazz too. Going out would invariably involve music, it stirred both our souls. We bought every single Elton John ever recorded and we used to pay four shillings to go to the Promenaders Gallery when the Proms were on.

I put our names on the list for Glyndebourne. I knew it might take a while to be offered tickets but I really fancied the whole long dress and posh picnic basket experience. We were on the list for four years but I never heard a thing.

****

My father had been forced to stop work. He was 53 and oxygen dependent. Emphysema had taken over the lungs that had been filled by roll-up smoke for a lifetime. As he became increasingly fragile, my mother had to give up work to care for him. Christine had finished her teacher training and landed a job in the North of England where her fiancé Pete was from. They were due to marry imminently. Only Tina was still putting money on my parents' table every week and she was counting the days to her twenty-first birthday when she could marry her childhood sweetheart.

The gravy train that had served Flora so well was coming to an end. They should have had a significant nest egg seeing as they both always worked and hadn't shouldered the expenses of bringing up their three children, but Flora was pleading poverty from the start.

Eventually, as Gerard became incapable of going anywhere unless the ground was completely flat, they were given a semi-disabled ground floor apartment.

Despite his wheezing, my father hadn't lost his ability to make my flesh crawl. We went down to see their new place with its light switches in the right position for a wheelchair user and rails around the bathroom. He didn't need to have a wheelchair as he just sat in his armchair all day long.

I was wearing a wine-coloured shift dress with a belt and very high shoes and stockings as we were going on to a concert afterwards.

"That dress is a lovely colour," my mother remarked.

"I think she looks lovely in that dress," Ken agreed, smiling at me.

"Yes, my Margy's always had a good arse!" the rasping voice from the corner added. I wanted to spit on him.

****

The Home Office were advertising in the local paper for a part-time Clerical Assistant. Teresa was about to start at nursery school so I thought I would try for it. Tupperware was great, but I was beginning to yearn for something that stretched me a bit more. However, getting into the Civil Service takes a while because they check absolutely everything.

I got through all the interviews fairly quickly despite the fact that my father held an Irish passport and the IRA was beginning to get active. They also looked into my mother's family and I had to go to an oculist in Wimpole Street to have the operations on my eyes evaluated. Then I had to sit the exam.

Ever since the debacle of my Eleven Plus, exams have crippled me with nerves. As I had never subsequently practiced studying or sitting exams, due to my prompt entry into the working world, my anxiousness had only increased.

The examiner placed a book of questions in front of me and I instantly went to pieces. I couldn't even remember my name! I sat there feeling sick: "What have I done? Why am I here?" was going round in my brain as the words on the page became jumbled into gobbledegook. There were questions about politics, English, the country, the royal family, puzzles and maths – all of which I could have answered if I were sitting in an armchair with Mum Williams, but in the end I only managed to write "Margy" at the top of the paper and attempt a couple of questions on the first page.

I received a follow up letter saying that "unfortunately" I hadn't managed to complete the exam – understatement of the year! – but that they would be inviting me back for another attempt. I was staggered that they bothered, seeing as I couldn't even remember my surname!

I'm as bad at rejection as I am about being kept waiting. I think both of these things are throwbacks to the mornings when I waited at the window for my parents' car to come round the corner to take me to visit Peggy and Noel, and it never did. Consequently I was in two minds about taking the exam again at all.

"You're a bright girl Margy," Mum Williams said over a couple of custard tarts. "You won't be 'appy if you don't try your best."

So I went back, and managed to remember my name. I had a mantra in my head, "read slowly, read slowly" because whenever I get nervous I rush things and then what I read makes no sense at all. I made myself read the questions slowly and take it in, then if I couldn't answer something I left it and went back to it later. When you haven't finished a formal education it makes you scared that other people will see the holes in your knowledge – and I didn't want to admit to them.

I'm fairly sure the Home Office must have mixed up some papers. There's probably some other poor sod who was rejected and never understood why! Miraculously, after the second exam they contacted me to say I had passed!

Mum Williams was so proud of me, she propped herself up on the front gate and told every passing neighbour about it for about three days.

I began in the Public Enquiry Office where I was dealing with the public most of the time. Soon I was moved into Immigration.

Enoch Powell's "rivers of blood" speech a few years before had done nothing to stem the tide of immigrants from Commonwealth countries who were eager to settle in Britain. Every morning the queue would be curling around the building by the time I arrived at work. When Prime Minister James Callaghan offered an amnesty so that illegal immigrants could regulate their status it got far worse. The corridors at work were filled with boxes of files and we couldn't put our feet on the floor under our desks but had to rest them on the boxes. At that time we had to work Saturdays and Sundays, so there was lots of overtime, but it was completely manic.

****

Many people have forgotten that we had a referendum in 1975. There was plenty of debate going on in the press between the Leavers and the Remainers then too. Labour had campaigned on the promise of holding a referendum on our EEC membership, and this was sufficient to get true blue Tory Enoch Powell to change colours completely and team up with the likes of Tony Benn and Michael Foot. There were arguments made that remaining so close to Europe would put "the language of Chaucer and Shakespeare under threat", and plenty of other highly emotive suppositions. However on the 6th of June the country totally trounced the Leavers when over 65 per cent of the population voted "Yes" to continuing European membership.

"At least that's put a final end to that question then!" Ken said when he got home from the printing presses that had been running red hot all day.

We didn't lose Shakespeare's language, but it looks as if we'll still lose Europe - 40 years later.

****

I loved my job and we were feeling quite rich. Our little house had trebled in value in three years, but I still hated not having an inside toilet. So we moved to a bigger house that had one.

When I picked Teresa up from school we would often go down to see Mum Williams, Kath and Hilda. Sometimes we would walk over Duppus Hill to see Ivy, Marjory and Charlie. All of them loved Teresa as she toddled about, beautifully dressed, like a living doll.

One day she was dressed in her little red fur coat. It had a little red hood and gloves on a thread. We walked through the back garden and along the gate to the kitchen door of 21A. I had Teresa's hand and urged her forward as I knew how much all their faces would light up as she walked through the door.

“Go on darling, walk in …”

Somehow Cyril’s Alsatian was in the kitchen. In an instant it went for her, clawing right through the coat to her little chest.

Rage and fear took over. Without thought of what those slathering jaws could do to us, Kath and I flung the dog out of the door, slamming it shut as we began to tend to the terrified toddler. None of the dogs we had cared for would ever have behaved like that, but Cyril’s influence was rising as Nell’s strength was ebbing. Kath may have loathed him, but he was still a man, they would still bow to his will in some measure. However low he stooped, somewhere inside themselves they still believed that, as women, they were less worthy.

Nevertheless, things were beginning to change.

“I do like that Angela Rippon,” Mum Williams said when the newsreader came on the television one afternoon. “I thought I’d never get used to ‘aving a woman read the noos at the start, but she’s all right.”

Nell still had problems differentiating between factual and dramatic programmes. The line between truth and art had been blurry for her ever since television sets were invented, but now other things were becoming smudged in her mind as well. Physically she was frailer. A cold would leave her tucked up beneath the brown blanket on her sofa for days. She could still boss Hilda around and refuse to see a doctor, but if I went to sit with her three days running, she would often say, “Margy, don’t leave it s’long before you come again.”

Chapter 21

In January 1976 everybody was singing Bohemian Rhapsody after Queen's massive Christmas hit. "Is this the real life? Is this just fantasy ..."

Later in the month the IRA detonated 12 bombs in London, including one in Selfridges on Oxford Street. At the UK Passport Holders department of the Home Office, where I was working at the time, we were definitely living a "real life" and were highly nervous and working overtime. Morning and night we had to check beneath our cars with a mirror before opening the door and putting the key in the ignition, in case some extra explosive hardware had been added to the underside.

It was the year of The Heatwave. It needs capital letters because despite all the global warming there has not been a time since when most of the British Isles have had zero rainfall in July and August. Although most of us were enjoying finally getting tanned legs, the Government was becoming desperate as the reservoirs dropped to dangerous levels.

"Look Mum," I said passing the paper over to her, "they're telling us to 'Save Water, bath with a friend!'"

"That's disgusting that is! There'll be none of that in my 'ouse! What'll they think of next?"

Punk Rock – as it happened!

The young people with spiked hair in lurid colours, safety pins piercing their cheeks and hanging out of their ears and eyebrows, were slouching their way past Nell's gate as she sat looking at them, open-mouthed.

"There's got t'be summat wrong wiv them, Margy. Don't their Mums tell 'em those safety pins could get infected?"

Nell's life had spanned the prudery of Queen Victoria's empire, through two world wars - which had finally dispensed with the great houses she had served in as a young woman, to female emancipation, the abdication of a King for the love of an American divorcee, the abolition of the death penalty, the pill, legalisation of gay relationships, and now there were a bunch of brightly coloured, alien lookalikes parading through down her street. No wonder she was confused at times!

****

In December Hilda phoned me.

"Margy, Mum's had a really big stroke. The doctor's been down and 'e says not to move her. Can you come?"

When I arrived Nell was in Hilda's brown chair. Someone had moved a bed down from upstairs and it was squeezed into the front room. It was the bed that really struck me. I had never known Mum Williams lie down in a bed before. I went over to her but she didn't speak or look at me.

"She's sleeping Margy. She's worn out," Hilda said from somewhere within her tears.

Kath was visibly upset too. For once she didn't have a single comment to make towards Hilda. I was stunned. I kept saying to Hilda, "She'll be all right. It will all be all right…"

Other people kept arriving and talking in whispers.

The people dissolved into a peripheral background as I knelt down alongside the chair and took Nell's small head in the crook of my arm. I cuddled her towards me as Marjory and her grown up twins came in. As I looked up to speak to them, Nell gave a big sigh.

"Hilda?"

"I think she's gone Margy."

Flattened by the knowledge that I hadn't been able to stop her leaving, I began to dissolve from the inside out. My throat was flaming with the unvoiced screams I was choking back. My legs were pulped. My heart was hammering through my ribs. My mind, completely dismantled. I have no idea how I got home.

****

I had seen other dead people. It was standard practice. So I went to see Nell with Kath and Hilda. Cyril turned the corner as we were walking towards Shakespeare's funeral parlour.

"What's 'e doin' 'ere?" Kath cried, "Mum 'ated 'im all 'er life."

But he was already too close, and there was no way the women would bitch in front of a man. We eyed the bunch of red roses in his grubby hands. He looked as if he was going on a date.

"Glad I wasn't fucking late, let's get the fuck in there then. No good comes of putting off the fucking inevitable. Chin up."

He held open the door and we eased our way in.

My brain blocked them out, completely. All I could see was my Mum in a coffin. I couldn't believe I couldn't talk to her, I couldn't hug her, I couldn't make her smile.

I kissed her.

My lips didn't meet Sleeping Beauty. She wasn't there. It was like cold, hard marble. I would never do that again.

Cyril started throwing his red roses in the coffin and Kath walked out. In the street Kath grabbed Hilda to one side, "'ow dare 'e!" she hissed. "'ow dare 'e do that to our mother!"

Hilda was in tears. Kath was striding away in high dudgeon. There was no Mum to sort it out.

****

Ken and I opened the door of 21A. Charlie was in the kitchen.

"All the flowers are upstairs in Mum's room," he said, seeing our display.

I went upstairs expecting to see the familiar jumble of school cups and ribbons, the pedal organ and the framed photographs hanging from the picture rail. There was nothing - just the carpet and several wreaths. All the knickknacks, the carefully boxed toy sets, the best china and the Christmas glasses, had vanished. The walls were adorned only with pale square patches on the paper where the photographs had hung. I was already numb. I only felt "Why?"

A shout went up, "Mum's here … she's here …" and the Shakespeare boys came in to collect all the wreaths.

"Hello Miss, I never thought I'd see the day your Nan died," and he went back down the stairs with an armful of flowers.

It seemed such a strange thing for an undertaker to say, but I guess Nell had been there so long, and she always seemed to be such a strong woman – despite the bandy legs – that a lot of people might have felt like that. Apart from the crash which killed Nell's husband, there was never a whiff of scandal about the family. Not once had a policeman ever come to our door, except for a cup of tea. The neighbourhood respected the lady who had taken care of so many of their children over so many years. The Old-Witch-on-the-corner never asked for anything back. If she could help, she would. If she couldn't, she'd get one of her daughters to do it!

It was wet and windy outside and the ground was slippery in Croydon cemetery as Nell's coffin was lowered into the grave beside her beloved Albert. As we drove away, teardrops of rain streaked down the windows and I thought, "She's going to be so cold. How can we leave her there? She'll be frozen."

At the house they were all abustle with sandwiches and tea. Relieved voices started filling the front room: "It was a nice do wasn't it … did you see the flowers … lovely … she would have loved it wouldn't she …" and all I could think was, "No, she wouldn't have loved it, she'd want to be here with us."

After Nell died I went through a dark few years. I don't think even Ken knew how low I became. It wasn't just losing Mum Williams herself, although that was the largest part of it. Everything else started to melt away too. There was no need to go to 21A now that she wasn't there.

The family splintered. My sisters and I naturally gravitated to our favourites and that was as far as further contact went. Christine was closest to Kath - although now that she had moved north we saw little of our middle sister. Tina had a special relationship with Hilda who had been most instrumental in bringing her up as Mum Williams had become very arthritic by the time she was born. I adored Ivy, the calmest one who always tried to pour oil on troubled family waters.

****

I may have been struggling inside but I still loved my job. I was promoted and given a side step into the Deportation Department. It was the complete opposite of Immigration, but even busier. Some days you would run into the office at 9am and not manage to take your coat off until 10.30am because the phones were ringing non-stop.

The appeals were a bit of a joke. It took ages to exhaust them all because the Home Office actually paid for the social workers and lawyers in UKIAS – the UK immigration assistance body – who were working against the HO's wishes! If someone finally did get deported, Britain used to pay to transport all their goods and chattels back to their country of origin too. In the courts you could spot the social workers a mile off – all dressed in beads and Indian sandals with the "Hey Man" hippy look!

A few of the immigrants were quite clever and used to get their local MP involved – even though he wasn't really their local MP because they had no right to stay in the country. Most of the MPs used to jump on the bandwagon. Time and again we'd have a guy on an aeroplane and then would have to get him off because an MP had got involved. It could be very frustrating.

Members of the Deportation Department frequently had to go to court to give a witness statement on behalf of the Home Office. The first time this happened to me I was sent to Salford near Manchester. Whoever was going would phone the local police before leaving to get all the arrangements straight. The police liked us and were often quite cheeky. I needed to identify the policeman when I arrived so I asked him, "Will you be wearing your uniform?"

"No, I'm actually off that day, but if you hear a pair of high heels clicking down the station, that will be me! Are you nervous?"

"I am so nervous! What happens if I mess this up?"

"You'll be absolutely fine. We'll settle you into your hotel and then you'll come out with us for a meal and in the morning we'll give you plenty of time to speak to our brief and he'll know everything about the Immigration Act and will put your mind at rest."

When the morning came I was too nervous to eat breakfast and I couldn't call home for some reassurance as there were no mobile phones so you tended not to call unless it was an emergency. A police car arrived and collected me. I was shown into an office, my papers held stiffly beneath my arm.

There was a very young man with black hair and a grey suit sitting awkwardly behind a desk. He jumped up and stuck out his hand before blurting out,

"Am I glad to see you! I don't know anything about the Immigration Act!"

Thank god it was adjourned.

Afterword

Soon after Mum Williams passed away, Cyril moved into 21A with Hilda and the vicious dog. This was more than Kath could stand. Her friend Violet was a widow by then, so the two of them bought a house together and moved down to Barnstable. Finally 21A got a shower room – where the scullery had been – and an indoor toilet when they knocked the wall down between the outdoor loo and the scullery.

****

It was a Friday afternoon in 1982, and I was working full time at Luna House in Deportation, when the phone rang.

"Hello Margaret, it's your mother, your father died today."

I hadn't spoken to him or seen him for at least two years.

"Are you all right?"

"Well, I'm shook up, I was shopping when 'e went. Naturally I need some help."

"All right, I'm due to leave in a few minutes. I have to go home to sort out Teresa and then I'll come down." I didn't feel a thing.

Teresa was 11 years old. She had just started senior school and would come home with the neighbour's children. She would let herself into our house at 4.05 and I was always home by 4.30. By the time I arrived, Teresa was crouched on the doorstep crying her eyes out. My mother had put the phone down to me and instantly phoned the house to tell Teresa that her grandfather had died. Although Teresa wasn't close to him it was her first real brush with death and she was in a house on her own. She opened the front door and sat on the step so that she didn't feel alone as she knew I would be coming down the road at any minute. Why my mother felt the need to do that, I have no idea!

I brought Flora home with me that night and she stayed with us until after the funeral. The first day after Gerard's death we took Flora to the undertakers to make arrangements. Immediately she said, "I haven't got any money."

"What about your daughters?" the hushed tones of the undertaker asked. "Could they contribute?"

"No, sorry, can't afford it," came straight out of my mouth. Tina said the same.

"We'll think about it," Flora said and, holding her head high, strode out of the premises.

"Are you sure you haven't got anything to contribute?" she prodded when we got outside. "I'm a poor widow now and you know how religious your father had got in his final years, he wanted a full wake and all. It would be a shame not to grant his dying wishes …"

"Haven't got a penny."

"Well…" she pondered, "I've got some money in the Abbey. It won't stretch to anything fancy though."

So we took her down to the Abbey National and we had to sit down and wait. We instinctively knew we couldn't go up to the desk with her. We weren't meant to see how much she had. As she pushed the book over the counter she turned round and looked at us.

"Oh, I feel a bit faint," she said, swaying slightly.

"That'll be because she's got to use some of her own money," Tina growled.

Flora put the deposit down and the rest had to be paid before the actual day. It was as cheap as possible, no cars, no wake.

My sole input was to make sandwiches to take over for the people who would come back to the house. I arrived at the door, which was opened by Christine.

"Where's Mum?"

"At the hairdressers," I rolled my eyes. "The neighbour came in yesterday and gave her ten pounds, I think it was for flowers because the neighbour can't come, but Mum decided it was so she could treat herself!"

I could just imagine Flora saying it: "I 'ad to tret myself, what wiv all I've been through this week!"

Peggy and Noel arrived plus some of the rest of the Irish family. Then there was Elsie who also lived in the complex and with whom Flora became friendly.

I wasn't wearing black. Not a chance. I felt total relief when he died and on the day of the funeral the only emotion I experienced was "Come on, let's get this done." The one thing that concerned me was seeing Christine so upset. She sobbed. I think she missed him. She laid claim to the chair he had spent so many years sitting in and had it re-upholstered and installed in pride of place in her house. She loved him and mourned him. I wish I could have felt like that, it would have meant that so much else had been different.

****

Kath developed cancer in 1990. Violet had already died. When Kath was very ill she decided she wanted to return to the family home for her final days. Marjory and I drove down to Barnstable. We wrapped Kath up in an eiderdown and brought her back to Croydon in the back seat of my car. When we got to the Mitcham Road Kath woke up.

"Are we nearly home Margy?" she said in barely a whisper.

"Nearly, we're on the Mitcham Road."

"Why have we stopped?"

"I'm just getting a bit more petrol. We'll be there very soon."

She died at 21A two weeks later, and was laid to rest in the same plot as her mother and father.

****

Flora remained in the ground floor flat after Gerard died. She became diabetic and her kidneys weren't good but she was all right until she had a bout of heart problems after the doctors took her thyroid out in 1992. Later she very suddenly lost her mind and was sent to the local asylum until doctors discovered it was due to potassium leaking into her blood stream. Once this was rectified she was lucid again, but her kidneys were failing and she had pneumonia and bronchitis. The doctors told me she wouldn't last much longer. Marjory and Ivy came up to the Mayday to visit so I went home and phoned Christine and Tina. Then I made a large flask of tea and a load of sandwiches. Marjory, Ivy and I stayed with Flora all night, just chatting and holding her hand.

Teresa came up to the hospital that evening but as soon as she saw her she began to cry.

"Don't do that darling because she can still hear you, just talk to her."

So Teresa got herself together and touched her arm, "You all right Nanna? It's Teresa."

Flora opened her eyes, "Hello Teresa." Then she closed them and went back to sleep.

She died in the early hours of the morning.

Flora's funeral was on the 26th November. Christine was in the kitchen making a cake especially for Ken. Christine is a genius at baking and Ken was fully appreciative of her skills. All the family got on well with Ken, and as the three of us stood there with our respective husbands, nobody could guess that within five months Ken would have also gone – it was the loss of Ken that eventually led me to leave for Spain and meet my wonderful second-husband, Esteban.

We gave Flora a good send off. Each of us stood up and said something. I read the poem "Footsteps". It's about going through life's troubles and of being carried through them either by God or a loved one. I have no idea why I read it.

Christine and I gave Elsie a lift back to the complex after the funeral. She was a lovely old soul, probably rather lonely as she never stopped talking for the entire drive.

"Oh I will miss your Mum … you'd never believe the fun we had at the cinema … you girls gave her a lovely service, she deserved that … used to go to the embroidery club every Wednesday, not that either of us were any good, but we had a laugh and Flora was such a wonderful person … you only get a friend like that once in a lifetime …"

We settled Elsie back in her flat and walked out to the car. I was quiet.

"Are you all right?" Christine asked.

"Yes, I'm just wondering who she was. After what Elsie said, I'm not sure I knew her at all."

****

Music still has the power to move me like nothing else on earth, but music can't explain the selfless soul that was Nell Williams.

This book is my hymn of thanks to a woman who would have made a wry comment at any suggestion that she was worthy of universal admiration. Largely uneducated and filled with stiff Victorian ideas - some of which led her to make decisions that would be censured today - she makes an unlikely heroine. Yet without her, four baby girls, and countless South Croydon families, would have encountered a life far less rich in love.

Nell Williams may not have always been right, but she was
unfailingly kind.

For photos and more information about some of the places and characters in this book, visit The Shadow Of The Teapot Facebook page.

The Smuggler's Song - *by Rudyard Kipling*

If you wake at midnight, and hear a horse's feet,
Don't go drawing back the blind, or looking in the street,
Them that ask no questions isn't told a lie.
Watch the wall my darling while the Gentlemen go by.

Five and twenty ponies,
Trotting through the dark –
Brandy for the Parson, 'Baccy for the Clerk.
Laces for a lady; letters for a spy,
Watch the wall my darling while the Gentlemen go by!

Running round the woodlump if you chance to find
Little barrels, roped and tarred, all full of brandy-wine,
Don't you shout to come and look, nor use 'em for your play.
Put the brushwood back again – and they'll be gone next day!

If you see the stable-door setting open wide;
If you see a tired horse lying down inside;
If your mother mends a coat cut about and tore;
If the lining's wet and warm – don't you ask no more!

If you meet King George's men, dressed in blue and red,
You be careful what you say, and mindful what is said.
If they call you "pretty maid", and chuck you 'neath the chin,
Don't you tell where no one is, nor yet where no one's been!

Knocks and footsteps round the house – whistles after dark –
You've no call for running out til the house-dogs bark.
Trusty's here, and *Pincher's* here, and see how dumb they lie
They don't fret to follow when the Gentlemen go by!

If you do as you've been told, 'likely there's a chance,
You'll be give a dainty doll, all the way from France,
With a cap of Valenciennes, and a velvet hood –
A present from the Gentlemen, along 'o being good!

Five and twenty ponies,
Trotting through the dark –
Brandy for the Parson, 'Baccy for the Clerk.
Them that asks no questions isn't told a lie –
Watch the wall my darling while the Gentlemen go by!